THE ROAD TO VILLA PAGE

*A He Said/She Said Memoir of
Buying Our Dream Home in France*

—{ BOOK ONE }—

CYNTHIA ROYCE
WILLIAM JAMES ROYCE

Mechanicsburg, PA USA

Published by Sunbury Press, Inc.
Mechanicsburg, Pennsylvania

www.sunburypress.com

Copyright © 2019 by Cynthia Royce & William J. Royce.
Cover Copyright © 2019 by Sunbury Press, Inc.

Sunbury Press supports copyright. Copyright fuels creativity, encourages diverse voices, promotes free speech, and creates a vibrant culture. Thank you for buying an authorized edition of this book and for complying with copyright laws by not reproducing, scanning, or distributing any part of it in any form without permission. You are supporting writers and allowing Sunbury Press to continue to publish books for every reader. For information contact Sunbury Press, Inc., Subsidiary Rights Dept., PO Box 548, Boiling Springs, PA 17007 USA or legal@sunburypress.com.

For information about special discounts for bulk purchases, please contact Sunbury Press Orders Dept. at (855) 338-8359 or orders@sunburypress.com.

To request one of our authors for speaking engagements or book signings, please contact Sunbury Press Publicity Dept. at publicity@sunburypress.com.

ISBN: 978-1-62006-257-9 (Trade paperback)

Library of Congress Control Number: 2019953529

FIRST SUNBURY PRESS EDITION: January 2020

Product of the United States of America
0 1 1 2 3 5 8 13 21 34 55

Set in Adobe Garamond
Designed by Crystal Devine
Cover by Terry Kennedy
Edited by Erika Hodges

Continue the Enlightenment!

To Jacques & Christiane
Nos Beau Voisins

Villa Page
Relais de Chasse/Hunting Lodge

HIS INTRODUCTION

If you're like me, you've often dreamed of owning a home in a quaint little village in one of the most idyllic spots in all of France. The only difference is, I actually own one . . . It's a long story, got a minute?

Technically, this story began several years ago. After finding our beautiful 200-year-old golden stone home on the Dordogne River in South-West France, our *notaire* (similar to a lawyer, but with a lot more power) informed us that he knew an *architecte* who could inspect it for us. *Parfait*.

Unfortunately, we arrived twenty minutes late to discover Jean-Pierre, the architect, leaving the property. Surely, a four-bedroom, two-story home and a seven-bedroom guest house with three kitchens and three bathrooms would take more than twenty minutes to examine.

"Je ne sais pas pourquoi je suis ici," said Jean-Pierre with a thick Southern French accent. I looked over at the English-speaking *immobilier*, real-estate agent, who translated for me.

"He says he does not know why he is here."

I turned to Jean-Pierre. *"Vous êtes ici examiner la maison,"* I replied in my worst high school French.

"Oui," he said, knowingly.

"Oui. Have you? Uh, *avez-vous?"*

"Oui," he replied.

"And?" I reached back twenty years and came up with, *"Qu'est-ce que . . . vous pensez?"* (What do you think?)

"Je ne sais pas pour quoi je suis ici."

Again, I looked at the *immobilier*, and again he informed me that Jean-Pierre had no idea why he was there.

After a couple more rounds of this, Jean-Pierre proclaimed the home to be in good condition.

"*Oui?* It's in good condition?" I said with equal parts relief and skepticism. As Jean-Pierre lit up another little brown cigarette, I asked him about the creaking, two-hundred-year-old staircase.

Jean-Pierre nodded thoughtfully. *"L'escalier est vieux et fatigué."*

My French was slowly coming back to me. "The staircase is old and tired?" I turned to the *immobilier* in disbelief. "That's his professional opinion? It's old and tired?"

Jean-Pierre may not have spoken English, but he understood that I was questioning his authority. He exhaled, dropped the freshly-lit brown cigarette on what was to become my new walkway and informed me, while grinding it out with his hand-crafted leather shoes, that he would be putting his official stamp on the inspection report, and that was that. End of discussion. The official stamp, I was soon to learn, is a powerful thing in France. Who was I to question Jean-Pierre's official stamp?

Standing there, looking down at that smoldering cigarette, I began to wonder what in the world I was doing buying *une maison ancienne* in the heart of Périgord Noir. How did this happen? How did I get here?

Her Introduction

Okay, first of all. I have to say, "No! I never dreamed of owning a home in a quaint little village in the south of France." Looking back, however, there was a pivotal moment when I could have said . . . "I don't think so!"

We were on vacation. It was so beautiful, so romantic, and out came those fateful few words . . . "Honey, why can't we live here?" Well, a vacation is one thing, but moving to France was an entirely different bouillabaisse! (Kettle of fish, get it?) As a girl from Memphis, I had already jumped a few hurdles of acceptable crazy behavior from my family when I moved to California. "That's where all the fruits and nuts come from," is a saying my Uncle Buddy might have coined.

So, how did I let this happen? Now, that's a good one. Let's see . . . I loved my husband. I wanted to get out of Los Angeles. I wanted an adventure. I was beginning to think my French wasn't so bad. Ha! Oh, we Americans are a confident bunch, aren't we?

I'm sure some of you have been there; in bed at night, or over dinner, listening to talk of dreams long harbored, adventures long sought after, a craving for a better life. But France?! What about—oh, I don't know—Canada? It's a lot closer. Or Northern California, for that matter? I know, not as daring, not as . . . crazy?

We were ready for a change, an adventure. Our lives together, almost ten years, had always been an adventure, so why stop now?

I am not promising a bed of roses, as all dreams from dreamers have thorns, but we had a dream, or at least one of us did. For me, it was more of a *Well, I'm willing to follow your dream.* It may not have been my dream, but fortunately, I was up to the task of getting us packed and on that plane to France.

—{ HIS STORY }—

CHAPITRE UN

"Have you ever thought of dyeing your temples?" the executive producer asked me in passing. It was code, but it wasn't cryptic. At thirty-nine, with graying temples, my days were numbered as a writer for prime-time network television. Roughly three hundred and sixty-five. Although I was behind the camera and not in front of it, I was quickly approaching the wrong demographic.

Every year, younger and hipper was getting younger and hipper. At thirty-nine, I could see the writing on the wall. In fact, at thirty-nine, I could still write on that wall, but I was seventy-eight in writer years. I may not even be able to see the wall in a couple years. It hadn't been a long career, but what it lacked in length, it more than compensated for with stress and money.

So, at forty, I fired my gardener, raised the salary to $50,000 a year and took the job myself. I had finally found my true calling. I wasn't just a leaf-blower, oh no. I installed a fountain, a koi pond, and built a stone wall, hand-selecting each stone and mixing my own mortar—nine hundred pounds!

While I was thinking of giving myself a raise, my wife had thoughts of her own. At forty, she wanted to start a family. After a year of charting temperatures and discarding dozens of EPT and ovulation kits, we were no closer to having that precious little bundle. Well, we may've missed one golden opportunity when I was almost arrested. It was the right night, at the right time, with the candles glowing and soft music playing. Before things got too hot and heavy, our dog started barking in the yard.

I quickly got up, fumbled my way through the darkness, entered the security code to de-activate the system, and called the dog inside. I climbed back into bed and again, just before the moment, we were interrupted. This time, it was the doorbell. The dog, naturally, began to bark ferociously. I glanced at the clock; it was after midnight. Who would drop in unannounced at this hour?

"It's the police!"

The police? Although I had done nothing wrong, a healthy dose of fear raced through my veins. The police don't just come banging on your door in the middle of the night for nothing.

As my wife tried to stop the dog from barking, I called out from behind the heavy front door.

"What do you want?"

Again the voice claimed to be the police. Over the barking, I couldn't hear the rest. I, too, yelled at the poor dog to stop barking. When I looked through the peephole, I couldn't see anyone on the porch. They were purposely standing out of my vision. Maybe they weren't the police at all, I thought.

"Open the door!" came the command.

"No!" my wife yelled at the dog.

"What do you want?" I repeated to the unseen stranger on my porch.

"We're responding to an emergency call."

"An emergency call? We didn't call you."

"Sir, open the door right now."

"But you're at the wrong house! Hurry! This is an emergency! Someone called you and you're wasting time standing here on my doorstep!"

"We are not at the wrong house, sir. Now, open that door."

I looked over at my wife, dressed in her sexy teddy, keeping the dog at bay. "I guess I better open the door. Maybe you should wait in the bedroom."

I opened the door to find two officers, male and female, weapons drawn, standing on my front porch. "We received an emergency alarm signal from this residence."

"An emergency alarm signal? I don't even know what that means."

"We need to see everyone in the home."

My wife came out in her robe and, together, we learned that our security system had a special little feature: If you enter the code with the last digit one number higher, you've sent a secret alarm to the police. We learned this, but not until after I was interrogated for possible spousal abuse. Needless to say, by the time we got back to bed, it was impossible to recapture the mood.

After a year, we decided to go through the whole fertility doctors rigmarole. I say we, but my role really hadn't changed much. Aside from the fact that my part now took place in a hospital bathroom with a VCR, porno tapes, and a little plastic cup. My part was a breeze, except for the time I had to race from a doctor's office in Beverly Hills to a hospital room in Century City with a rapidly expiring sperm sample on the passenger seat.

Then, one night, while lying in bed, my wife suggested adoption. So, we stumbled down that path instead. Now that we were, eventually, going to bring a child into our home, we realized that we didn't want to raise a child in Los Angeles. After all, we only moved here to work in film and television. Since we were no longer in "the biz," we were free to raise our child anywhere. But where? Where could we give our child the life that we had as children? Where could they grow up running free and happy with clean air, no trash, graffiti, violence, or metal detectors at the high school? Where could they go off for the day to play with their friends and we wouldn't have to worry about their safety?

―{ HER STORY }―

~~CHAPITRE DEUX~~ CHAPTER TWO

Forty?! I wasn't a day over thirty-seven! I had always planned on starting the baby-making process a whole lot earlier, but... We had a seven-year courtship before we could agree to get married. "Why get married? Why ruin a good thing?" spouted Bill. Really, men need to come up with some new material on the subject. "Okay, as long as it doesn't change anything."

"It won't," I lied.

Actually, I can't blame Bill for most of the delay. I had to go and get myself a career. Well, a ten-year stint as a TV writer. It all began one fateful day; while sick with strep throat, I got a call to interview for the position as an Executive Assistant for Carroll O'Connor, whom some of you will know best under the name Archer Bunker, the star and new executive producer of *In the Heat of the Night*. For those of you not familiar, the series was based on the Academy Award winning movie with Rod Steiger and Sidney Poitier. My southern heritage came in handy on that one; set in a small town in Mississippi, O'Connor played a chief of police, paired with a fish-out-of-water black cop, portrayed by the immensely talented Howard Rollins.

For Carroll, the fact that I was from the south and had actually been raised outside of Atlanta, close to where the show would be filming, was enough to hire me as his assistant. I had been working in Hollywood for five years and had a lengthy resume. I had nine jobs by the end of my first year. Actually, the two highlights were working for Noel Marshall, producer of *The Exorcist*, when his new company went bankrupt. He kept me and my friend on salary in an empty office to answer phone calls from creditors and disgruntled employees whose checks were bouncing. When I quit to move onto my ninth job, my friend called me a traitor. Oy! The last job that year was working at NBC Studios as a page, for which I was royally paid less than minimum wage, worked only twenty-five hours a week, and had to have a degree for the job! Ah, Hollywood . . .

But, I digress.

Little did Carroll know that within nine months from my interview, the show would be in production on an episode written by me and Bill. They ran into script trouble when co-star Howard Rollins went into the hospital and the company was going to have to shut down. Bill and I had been working on a spec script and handed it to Carroll. The other executive producer, Fred Silverman's only comment was, "Is it in English?" This was the stamp of approval we needed for the script to get the green light and start filming—before we were even paid!

I will never forget the pivotal moment of sitting across from Carroll in his robe and slippers, his hair à la Einstein, at his condo in Georgia. We were discussing the stories that were coming down the pike and I handed him our story for a new episode.

Carroll gave me a stern look over his specs, "I do not want to lose a good secretary to the script department."

From the other room came the commanding voice of his wife, Nancy O'Connor. "Carroll O'Connor you cannot do that. You cannot keep her from moving forward."

Thank you, Nancy! And Carroll, of course. For although he was very stubborn and a pain in the ass in so many ways, I loved him dearly and he changed our lives forever.

Carroll, Bill, and I shared a production trailer in Covington, Georgia. One day, he brought us into his office and told us that we would be hired as story editors and that it would change our lives. We would buy a house, he informed us. We not only bought a house because of Carroll, we sold that house and bought our new home in France.

I was promoted to story editor and, because Carroll did not believe writers should be producers, eventually rose to the title of executive creative consultant. Bill and I wrote more than thirty shows. We were lucky to be on staff for one of the last shows to be sold into network syndication, the residuals giving us a golden mailbox, as they say. Those magic green envelopes were manna from heaven, because you never knew when they were coming or how much they would be. It was a life-saver for us. After my brief career as a TV writer, Bill turned forty, and our writing days for prime time were ending.

When I was in the thick of it, working sixty to seventy-hour weeks, it didn't leave a lot of stress-free time for taking your temperature and charting your cycles, let alone getting a good night's rest. So, after three tries at the in-vitro fertilization merry-go-round, I found myself in a hormone haze and ready to try something else. An egg donor?!

"She's cute. She looks like you." Bill said as he was looking at the donor website.

"No, she doesn't. And she's not that cute." I objected.

Trying to decide on a candidate from whom we would buy their eggs wasn't going to be easy. It was probably better to conceive like those who used sperm banks and aren't able to put a face with the eggs. Or, knowing their favorite movie or book, for that matter.

At one point, Bill's old girlfriend actually offered her eggs. Which, oddly enough, was no big D to me at first. Then it dawned on me: Hey, she's only two years younger than me. Not to mention, it could create a rather unique situation. Would our child have two mommies? Would my daughter look like Bill's old girlfriend?

While we were trying to decide what our next step would be, I saw the film *Cider House Rules*. I'm sure John Irving had no idea that one day a hormone-crazed woman would see his film and it would change her life, many lives actually. Why spend thousands of dollars to buy someone else's eggs, get back on the in-vitro merry-go-round with the possibility of being disappointed again when there were so many children in the foster care system who needed adopting?

During the whole adoption process, running away to France was like a breath of fresh air, literally. My French being better made me the go-to guy, or "gal," in this instance. Ah, the French countryside, the cheese, the wine, and those beautiful accents. It was all so romantic and, for a photographer, a photo-op at every turn. The more I traveled, the more I got the photo bug. In fact, it was France that first inspired me to become a photographer. My wedding gift was a Canon Rebel from my new husband for our trip to Paris.

I never was inspired to shoot in LA, except for in the studio and the occasional portrait. I had taken an inspiring class in Santa Fe, which I got into by submitting my portfolio. When I arrived, I felt completely overwhelmed by the other students, who turned out to be professional photographers. It was a great workshop and I followed it with another one in Cuba at a time when Americans were denied access to the intriguing island and its captivating images. France, however, became my favorite subject. Well, one of them, at least.

Anyway, I digress yet again.

So, making a baby wasn't in the stars for us. Growing up, I had always thought I would have several children. The path to adoption is never an easy one, whether it is private, international, or through foster care. But when you want a child, none of it matters until you have one. They say that the soft cheek of a baby releases a scent when kissed that is the gift that keeps giving until the child is two years old; the perfect time to start planning the second child. I wanted a baby almost more than anything in the world. I wanted to kiss and coo over those irresistible cheeks and I couldn't help wondering if it would ever happen. Meanwhile, the clock was ticking and if we were ever to be so lucky as to bring our little bundle of joy home, where would that home be?

We were ready for a new adventure, one that didn't involve a big city like LA. I was never really a big city girl and wanted to give my children the kind of life I had, roaming the neighborhood with my friends and staying out after dark. That certainly wasn't in Los Angeles, but where? We considered Ashland, Oregon quite seriously. We met a real estate agent and visited Bill's friends who lived there. It was a cute and cultured little town, but step outside of Ashland and oh, boy! It was a bit scary. And then, it wasn't really France, was it?

―{ HIS STORY }―

CHAPITRE TROIS

We decided to give ourselves a vacation from the stress of conception, donor eggs, hormone shots, and adoption. On our honeymoon, Cynthia and I had gone to Europe for the first time. We enjoyed driving through rural France and Italy so much that we tried to go back every year thereafter.

While perusing the books in a travel section, I happened upon *The Most Beautiful Villages of the Dordogne*. I had never heard of this region of France. I opened the book to discover that these villages were not only the most beautiful of the Dordogne, but I dare say, of all of France. If a book ever changed anyone's life, this one surely changed mine.

Our first time through the region known as the Périgord was a whirlwind of fine hotels and Michelin starred restaurants. The hotels and the terrain seemed to become more and more beautiful the deeper we got into the Dordogne. Our first stop was Le Moulin de l'Abbaye in Brantôme, dubbed the Venice of the Périgord with its impressive network of bridges and waterways. From there, it was a short hop to a delightful attic apartment at the charming, vine-covered Le Vieux Logis in Trémolat. Then it was off to Hotel de L'Esplanade in the enchanting, walled village of Domme, with its spectacular vista of the Dordogne River and its verdant valley.

We entered L'Esplanade to find the proprietor, Mme. Gillard, giving violin lessons to several village children. After checking into our room, opening the windows and breathing the fresh air, we headed down to the restaurant for a delightful meal of local cuisine. Over that meal, it seemed as though time stood still. We felt for the first time in a long, long time that we were exactly where we belonged. The simple life of the region was permeating our bodies like osmosis. Just by being in this land that has been continually inhabited for thousands of years by generation after generation, our lives had somehow changed.

After that wonderful meal, we went back to our room and learned one of the most important lessons in South West France: There are no window screens, so you should never leave your window open with the lights on when you leave for supper. I opened the door to discover that the walls were moving! Literally, thousands of flying bugs had made their way into our room!

Madame Gillard was apparently used to morons like us. Unfortunately, the hotel was full, so she handed us a can of bug spray. While we waited for our room to air out—with the lights off—we sipped Grand Marnier on the terrace and wondered about life amongst all the castles, open-air markets, and cobblestone streets.

From Domme, it was off to Rocamadour, a spectacular, vertical village, spilling down the side of a steep cliff. This sacred spot was once a major pilgrimage stop along the Way to Compostela. People would travel from all over Europe to climb the 223 steps on their knees to reach the Gothic Chapelle Notre-Dame, with its mystical statue of the Black Virgin.

Finally, it was back to Paris and the prestigious Hotel Duc de St. Simon and a room so small we had to walk on the bed to pass each other. Paris, a city I had always loved, now seemed like a stop-over on the way home. That night over dinner at Than, our favorite restaurant in Paris, all we could think about was the Dordogne and when we could come back.

That fall we returned to the Dordogne. This time, however, we decided to rent a home on the river to actually experience life in our favorite area, Périgord Noir. We arrived at our rental home to discover it was on the river, all right, but it was also directly across a small road from the church. Every morning at six, we awoke to the deafening sound of bells. And, just in case we managed to sleep through them the first time, they were repeated. The bells rang every hour on the hour and once at the half-hour. Other than this, the trip was everything you could possibly ask for, *et plus*.

Although we could and did buy our bread from the local *pâtisserie*, and our vegetables at the open-air market in nearby Le Bugue, we discovered a super-market, *Intermarché*, which had everything but sour cream—an idea that makes no sense to our friend who is the chef and owner of the unsurpassable Moulin du Roc.

"*Sour* cream?" said Alain, shaking his head at the notion. In France, where the *crème* is *fraiche,* along with the produce and the herbs and anything else in the meal, the idea of *sour* cream made absolutely no sense at all. And, in America, do you also drink curdled milk and eat stale bread?

Staying there in our rental home in Allas-sur-Dordogne, we realized for the first time that it was actually possible to live in rural France. Although there were no theaters showing the latest movies, and there certainly was no Thai food to be found this side of Paris, it was easy to imagine our lives there. Minus the bells!

As a lark, we decided to contact a British real estate agent named Delia to show us a few possibilities. We had arranged to meet her in the nearby village of Allas-les-Mines. Having made a wrong turn, we arrived in the deserted little village a bit late. As we pulled in, we saw an attractive woman getting into her car. I called out, "Delia?" and waved to stop her.

The woman smiled, said, "*Non*," but waived back in a very friendly manner.

Figuring we had missed Delia, we decided to explore the sleepy little village. My wife, being a photographer, was fascinated by the ruin of an old hotel/café. What had once been an attractive little enterprise was now a shell of beautiful golden stones, two stories high, with a tree growing inside. Cynthia loved the image and proceeded to set up her tripod in order to take the shot.

I looked over and saw an elderly woman sitting on a bench in the shade by the side of the church. She was watching our every move. I smiled, nodded in respect and said, "*Bonjour, Madame.*" I had learned the simple trick of including the '*Madame*' on every greeting. It worked. She smiled and wished me good day.

Just as my wife had finished, the lady I had mistaken for Delia returned. She introduced herself as Yanette and informed us that the café was *à vendre*.

"*À vendre, à vendre,*" I repeated, as if by repeating them I would discern their true meaning.

Yanette watched me struggle a moment and then searched her limited knowledge of *anglais* and said, "To buy?"

"Oh, it's for sale."

"*Voilà!*" she replied with a smile.

"The café is for sale," I said to my wife, who looked at me like I was quite nuts, indeed.

"*Oui,*" said Yanette, "*Et deux maisons, aussi.*"

"*Deux maisons* . . . two houses, also," I replied, quite proud of my translation of this difficult phrase.

Yanette proceeded to show us the two little homes that were included in the deal. When I was informed that the price was only $20,000, my curiosity was piqued. That night, over a fantastic bottle of dirt-cheap Bordeaux, I began to dream of restoring the old café. It had once been the heart of Allas-les-Mines. Now, there was nothing. No *pâtisserie*, no *tabac*, nothing. It's as though when that fire burned the Café Sauve Terre, it took the life from that little village.

The next day we returned to find Yanette and the elderly madame on her bench. This time, however, Madame approached us.

"*Vous allez acheter le café?*" she asked me.

Was I going to buy the café? Was I going to restore it? Was I going to bring life back to her village? Could I possibly restore her memories of laughter and drinks and good times in that bar? Would there once again be music and gaiety in Allas-les-Mines?

Suddenly, I was surrounded by local ladies, all wondering the same thing. Had this *Americain* come to restore the spirit of our village? I climbed through the missing window and stepped out the measurements, writing them down on my pad. My dream was now taking on the dimensions of a quest, a mission.

I looked up through the missing ceiling at the walls of the second floor. It once contained several hotel rooms and their bathrooms. Although the fire had consumed the ceiling and the roof, the beautiful tile of the showers and their antique hardware were still visible. We had thought of leaving the roof off, as well as leaving the indoor tree, and turning the space into an open-air wine bar, *avec un jardin intérieur*. We'd haul in some plants, add a fountain or two, the water spilling into them from the showers upstairs.

Near the end of our trip, we came to feel as though the long-forgotten café was ours. We'd arrive in the evening, sip wine from the ruin behind the café, and watch the sun set over the fields, the light reflecting off the golden stones of the châteaux on the opposite hill. We discussed everything from the menu to the decor to the music. We'd even met the perfect hostess for our new wine bar, Yanette.

When we informed Yanette that we were leaving in a few days, she invited us to share a drink in the village across the river, the beautiful hill town of St. Cyprien. This being her second invitation, we knew we had to accept. Besides, we had a little business proposition to discuss.

"*Quelle heure?*" I asked.

"*Onze. C'est bon, oui?*"

"*Onze?*" I turned to Cynthia. "Yanette wants to meet at eleven in the morning."

"*Oui,*" stated Yanette with smile.

Wow, we are truly in France now, I thought. We're invited by a local French woman to imbibe an aperitif before noon. Yanette informed us in French where to meet her. As we headed back to our rental home (and the bells!) we pondered our luck. We had met a friendly French lush. Maybe she was the wrong person with whom to entrust a wine bar. As so often is the case, we both thought the other person was paying attention to the directions.

The next morning, we parked our car at the end or Rue Gambetta and walked down the main street of St. Cyprien, hoping Yanette would spot her two lost *Americain* drinking buddies. We walked past the quaint storefronts of a beauty salon, a pharmacy, and an antique shop when I spotted Yanette through a window across the street. She was standing behind the cash register of a *cave*, a liquor store. We were both relieved to learn that Yanette wasn't a lush, after all. She was a successful business woman.

We entered *Le Choix des Rois*, The Choice of Kings, and were greeted with kisses, introduced to her charming husband, Daniel, and served a spectacular aperitif made from roses. Yanette and Daniel seemed genuinely pleased to learn that we had decided to buy the café. We all drank a toast to our new neighbors.

We flew back to Los Angeles with the idea of returning in one month with our proposal to purchase the café and the two homes. Café Sauve Terre had burned down fifteen years ago and now belonged to the community. Yanette informed us that we had to make our proposal to the mayor, Monsieur Magimel, and the community would either accept or reject our offer.

A month later, we were back in Périgord Noir, this time renting a home in the small village of Enveaux, near the castles of Castelnaud and Josephine Baker's les Milandes. After unpacking, we were both anxious to visit "our" café. Again we were greeted by the ladies, but this time, Yanette gave us kisses, *bisous*, on the cheek!

The dream of re-opening Café Sauve Terre became something of an obsession for me back in Los Angeles. I wasn't sculpting a replica of it in the living room with mashed potatoes, but I had sketched and painted the interior garden/wine bar as part of our proposal for M. Magimel. We had seen the mayor several times, putting around Allas-les-Mines in his little, faded blue Citroen truck. Unlike everyone else in town—or the Périgord, for that matter—M. Magimel always seemed to be in a hurry.

In our proposal, we would have to describe, in detail, our plans for the new café. Would M. Magimel comprehend the idea of a chic wine bar in the remains of a ruin? Although we'd be bringing commerce back to the village, there was a chance the commune would reject our presentation. Still, we didn't allow that to stop our dream from sprouting wings and taking flight. The little house next to the café would be transformed into a *pâtisserie*/bookstore displaying art and crafts from the local artisans

We had seen numerous imaginative signs advertising the wares from glass-blowers, jewelers, sculptors, potters, and painters. So, one crisp November day we journeyed out to the nearby artist community of Meyrals. We followed a colorful series of signs—a paintbrush pointing the direction—to an artist's studio. After winding through the hills above St. Cyprien, we found ourselves at the studio, home, and gallery of Guy Weir, an eccentric watercolorist from Great Britain.

When we arrived, Guy Weir, or "Gee Vee-ay" as the French refer to him, was brewing tea in his little stone farmhouse. He invited us to enter his barn, which housed his studio and gallery. From this beautifully renovated farm compound, Guy ran a highly successful enterprise. Admiring his prints and his original pieces, we knew we had to have Guy's work on display in our gallery.

Guy entered the barn, tea cup in hand, greeted us and climbed the wooden stairs to the upper level, his workspace. Bravely, we followed him upstairs, introduced ourselves, and detailed our plans. At that time, there were no English bookstores, nor had the idea of a bookstore/coffee house been introduced to South West France. The concept appealed to him, but there seem to be one slight problem.

"Where did you say this would be? Allas-les-Mines?" Guy thought back. "I was there once. A long time ago. Twenty years or so. I ate at a dreadful little place."

Oh no, what were the odds? "The Café Sauve Terre?"

"I don't know, I've blocked it out. It was that miserable."

"Well," I ventured forward, "it was burned down—"

"I remember it was run by this awful little German man, or Austrian, whatever he was, it was a miserable experience and I never returned to Allas-les-Mines."

With that, Guy swallowed the last sip, stood, and invited us over to his home for a cup of tea. Well, I thought, we might not get his art in our gallery, but this promises to be an adventure. We entered Guy's cozy little home and were invited to sit in his *salon*, right off the kitchen. Now, what kind of tea would we like?

A quick glance around the room revealed Guy's main vice, tea. Oh sure, Guy enjoyed a fine glass of wine or three, but tea was his drug of choice. We followed Guy into the kitchen and studied the many canisters and boxes of rare and exotic teas.

Standing at the ancient stone sink, Guy glanced over his shoulder at me. "You know the Asian woman at the market in St. Cyprien?"

"Uh, no, I don't think so."

"I usually buy my tea from her. She has a wonderful selection. Oh," he said, brushing past me, reaching for a colorful old container, "You might like this. It's from Ceylon. I just bought this yesterday."

He opened the canister and held it out for us to sniff. I inhaled and experienced an aroma I had never smelled before. Guy seemed genuinely pleased that we wanted to try it.

Over that first pot, sitting around a cluttered coffee table, Guy told us the story of his life. He was born and raised in England in an upper-crust family. Guy spoke French at an early age, due in part to the fact that the family always employed French maids. Guy raised an eyebrow at the memory of one particular French maid.

Although Guy had been around the world numerous times, the Dordogne, to him, was the most beautiful spot on earth. The most beautiful spot with gourmet food and superior wine. He had lived there for over twenty years and, recently, his ailing mother had come to live with him, in her own little stone home. Earlier that day, his mother had one of her "spells." Because she had always been very theatrical, Guy confided to us, he never knew whether or not to react to her complaints. He had, just to play it safe, put in a call to her doctor in St. Cyprien. He'd be stopping by a little later.

Stopping by? A doctor who still makes house calls? It felt like the French version of Mayberry. America in the fifties. As Guy headed for the kitchen to boil water and select the next tea, he was interrupted by a knock on the door. It was opened to reveal Robert, a thin man in his mid-sixties, wearing a vest and a cap. Guy invited Robert to enter and introduced him to us as his neighbor.

Robert bred horses and had been quite successful as a horse trader. His persona of a simple country bumpkin was merely a rouse, Guy revealed. As a successful horse trader, Robert had to know how to play the game and how to win. Not to cast aspersions on Robert, but horse traders, according to Guy, were nefarious characters.

Robert apologized to us for interrupting.

"*D'accord*, Robert," Guy repeated every few minutes as Robert rambled on and on in rapid, incomprehensible French. I couldn't tell if Robert was apologizing for something or explaining some *catastrophe*. At one point, Robert seemed to get a bit agitated. Guy put a friendly hand on his bony shoulder and said, "*D'accord*, Robert, *d'accord*."

When Robert left, Guy picked up where he had left off, studying the many canisters. "Now, let's see, which tea would be suitable for the occasion?"

It was none of my business, I know, but I had to ask. "What was that all about?"

"With Robert?" Guy said, re-entering the sitting area. "You have to understand, it's a different way of life out here." He poured the last remaining drops of that amazing tea into my cup and headed back to the kitchen. "How does a Chinese black tea sound?"

"Fine," we both chimed in unison. With his back to us, standing at the stone sink, Cynthia mouthed to me: What was that all about?

Guy returned with a fresh pot of tea and set it down on the cluttered table in front of us.

"Robert is semi-retired now," said Guy. Then he added with a laugh, "Which means he only works from sun up to sun down! As I say, it's a different way of life. Robert is a very complex man. Don't let his persona fool you. His son is a doctor and his daughter is a lawyer in Paris."

I can't tell you how relieved I was to hear that. It was such a relief to know that a child raised in rural France could be a successful lawyer in Paris, if that's what they chose. I would later learn that every school in France was equal. All the children learned the same things and were given the same examination on the same day. But the quality of education was only a fleeting thought, what I really cared about was that mysterious exchange with Robert.

"So, was there something wrong?"

"With Robert? No, not really." He poured a spot of tea into his cup to check the color. "It's got a bit more time on it."

"We're studying French—"

"Oh, yes. It's a beautiful language, isn't it? Perhaps the most beautiful."

"But all I could get from your conversation was: Okay, Robert, okay."

THE ROAD TO VILLA PAGE

Guy laughed. "My vines have grown over Robert's wall. You see, he now has time to notice such things. It's not a problem. I'll trim them back." He picked up the ceramic pot. "Tea?"

Over the next couple of rounds, we discussed everything from Guy's adventures in India to the immigration of Eastern Europeans to southern France. Guy, the colorful eccentric painter, a complete stranger, had taken us in, made us tea, told us about his mother, his childhood, and expounded on his view of the typical *Périgordin* and their *joie de vie*, their love of life, the importance of their family, and their reverence for the land. The land of their ancestors. A concept, Guy pointed out, that we as Americans, with such a young country, couldn't fully comprehend.

The hour was growing late and Guy wanted to check on his mother. As he walked us back to our car, Guy told us that he would gladly display his paintings in our gallery. What's more, he would introduce us to the painter, Pascal Magis, whom Guy obviously held in high esteem.

As we pulled away, we saw Robert standing by the wall in question, a pair of pruning shears in his gloved hands. Guy saw him at about the same time. He looked back at us, smiled, and shook his head. We smiled back and waved good-bye. What had started out as a miserable failure had turned into a wonderful afternoon and a major coup for our future gallery.

We had arranged for a female British contractor to meet us and give us an estimate for the restoration before making our proposal. She examined the two homes and the café and informed us that, yes, one could pick up these properties for a song, but the restoration had the price-tag of producing a Broadway musical.

As we stood there in the shell of that café on that brisk November afternoon, we began to wonder about our future. We looked out at the hopeful faces of the villagers and decided not to make any decisions just yet. If we were going to buy the café, we had thought, we'd need a place to live while the restoration was taking place.

Surfing the net, I had found a home nearby, on the river, with what promised to be its own private island. Not only did it have an island, it had what the ad described as *gîtes*, self-catering rental units. What's more, this four-bedroom home with all its land, was easily half the price of a three-bedroom home on a quarter acre in Ashland, Oregon, our second choice.

The home even had its own name, Villa Page. As we turned into the long driveway and Villa Page came into view, a strange feeling came over me. It was as though I had been there before, as if I was coming home for the very first time.

It was at this point that the *immobilier* turned to us in the backseat of his Mercedes and said, "The Berteloots, they do not tell anyone they are to sell the home."

"Oh?"

"Madame Berteloot, she has not even told her brother."

"Okay."

"He does not know they are to sell the home."

Why was he telling us this? Although it struck us as odd, we did not understand the significance of it at all. We assumed it was yet another French custom that we would soon comprehend. As it turns out, Madame's brother was in the house at that very moment helping Monsieur Berteloot restore it. Were we supposed to act like we weren't there to inspect the home for purchase? Who was he going to think these two Americans were and why were they walking through his sister's house?

Madame Berteloot opened the door with a smile and welcomed us into the foyer. Looking past the stacks of sheetrock, ladders, and exposed electrical wiring, revealed many nice details, including antique black and white floor tiles and a stunning plaster relief on the wall of maidens in flowing gowns. Ushered through the mess, we were introduced to M. Berteloot and his *beau-frère* as they hung the ceiling in a huge room containing the kitchen, eating area, and family room, known in France as a *cuisine Americaine*.

We looked around and realized that the Berteloots were quickly removing the charm and character of the centuries-old home, covering the beams and the interior golden stones with sheetrock, hiding everything that we would be purchasing the house for in the first place.

Although the home would require considerable restoration, it was all there, including a *cave*, a basement for my wife's darkroom, a playground with swings and a slide for our child, three rental units for income, a large terrace overlooking the river, not to mention a private island. When you were done, you would have a pretty spectacular home.

That night we went back to our rental home in Enveaux to discuss the possibilities. Suddenly, the very thing that had brought us back to France one month later—the café—seemed like an after-thought. I could easily imagine a life in that home on the river. I could see children playing in the yard, exploring the island, and swimming in the river. My wife, as it turns out, needed a bit of convincing. I had become so excited about life in another country, exploring a new culture, that I failed to see that she didn't quite share my enthusiasm. Not yet, anyway.

We had seen the home on Friday. The following Friday we would be in Paris, and by Saturday we would be home. I had one week to make an offer, apply for a mortgage, and convince my wife that I knew what the hell I was doing!

―{ HER STORY }―

~~CHAPITRE QUATRE~~ **CHAPTER FOUR**

September 11th, that iconic date, happened four days after I turned forty. An auspicious year for many reasons; an act of terror that the world had never witnessed before caught us completely off guard. With the bad always comes the good; this year, our child would be born and we would buy a house in France.

I had the most amazing and wackiest surprise party of my life, organized by my closest friends. One of whom—and she will remain nameless—showed up outside of the house the night of the party about thirty minutes early. I saw her through the trees, out in the street, pacing back and forth, carrying flowers. She was dressed as if she was going to a party.

"Oh," she said nonchalantly when I came down the stairs. "I just wanted to deliver the flowers in person." Naïve me, I totally fell for it. How sweet, I thought.

We had a lovely dinner at my favorite restaurant, Cha Cha Cha's, and I was none the wiser until we arrived at the house. You could have heard a pin drop, but up the stairs, under the gate, I could see many pairs of shoes. (I know, dear friends, this is the first you are finding this out.) The jig was up! But I did a great job of acting surprised. It was an amazing party.

That was September 9th. Two days later, the world would never be the same. I found out about the attack in a photography class at Glendale College, which I was taking with a couple of friends. It didn't quite sink in until I was driving home and heard over the radio the horror of what had occurred. I opened the door and rushed to the TV, trying to explain to Bill, who was on his way out the door to play tennis. When we watched the footage on TV, it finally hit home.

What was reported in the news, of course, were all the other terrorist attacks all over the world. But America was safe, wasn't it? We somehow thought we were immune, above the other countries who had been violated, but not anymore. It was the beginning of terror alerts, Homeland Security, and the countless hours at airports, waiting to be searched, wanded, and puffed by those mysterious cylinders which take apart ions and put them back together, looking for who knows what exactly.

We had a trip planned to go back to the Dordogne a week later on the 17th of September. It was on American Airlines, one of the airlines used by the terrorist. The flight had been cancelled because it was nonstop from LA to Paris. Non-stop flights had been cancelled during this time because of the quantity of fuel the plane would be carrying. They changed the flight to a connecting flight the following day. We were really on the fence about going. What if something happened? Very few people were traveling, especially overseas. Everyone was on high alert. We, like everyone in America, were in a state of shock. Of course, there were those like my hair cutter, "Oh, that was there, not here in Los Angeles." What? As such a large country, there is so much division, even in times of crisis.

We decided that if we stayed home, the terrorists won. We had fallen in love with the Dordogne on our first visit and were actually contemplating a life there. (Well, at least Bill was!)

We got to the airport and were the only ones in line at American Airlines and were informed at the counter that Bill's passport had expired. We stared at the date on the passport in a daze. I got chills as I felt that this was an omen. We weren't supposed to go. As usual, we got little sleep the night before, so Bill went home and crashed. He told me that if I could get an appointment to renew his passport that day, wake him up. Two hours later we were in line at the Passport office. We rebooked the flight for the following day and went back home.

That night, we watched the tribute to 9/11 and saw the unforgettable poignant performance of Neil Young singing "Imagine." We held each other close and cried for our loss, our loss as a country, filled with the sadness that the country we had grown up in would never be the same again. The innocence, the naivety that we were safe, was only a dream.

Arriving at Moulin du Roc, a true Eden set on the banks of the Dronne River, we were exhausted and overwhelmed. We had left America behind but carried the devastation with us. A combination of jet-lag and mourning hit us hard and we crashed into the heaven of a firm French bed set under ancient hand-carved beams. Thanks to Karen Browne's travel book, we could not have chosen a better place to regroup, a former walnut mill, whose property spanned the sides of the Dronne River, connected by arched bridges and twisting paths through treasure-trove gardens.

The restaurant and hotel were inherited by Alain Gardillou, who has managed to keep his Michelin starred establishment afloat in the Périgord Vert. His training started at the apron strings of his mother, long considered the best female chef in France and one of the first women to receive the coveted Michelin star.

When the TV in our hotel room reported that there had been an explosion in Toulouse and they thought it was an act of terrorism, we were horrified; the nightmare was following us. But Alain and Maryse, his beautiful wife, nearly always dressed straight from the Paris runways, offered comforting words and solace. She explained the incident in Toulouse was only an accident.

People who say that the French do not like Americans are making an unfair generalization that I have to clear up right now. Which Americans and which French? I have never visited a hotel anywhere in the world and felt that two people opened their arms to us more than Alain and his wife, Maryse. She was one of my first French teachers in France, as her English was excellent, but she cajoled me into speaking French every chance she had.

We had booked three days at this enchanted hotel and had planned on exploring the countryside, but we spent the whole time at the hotel soaking in the beauty, the incredible gastronomic creations by Chef Alain, and soothing our troubled spirits. My photographic sensibilities quickly awoke after I got more than a few winks; it began with taking pictures out of our room's window at the exquisite river banks. From the window of our soon to be favorite room, which we requested during our many stays there,

I could see the whimsical island with its tiny gazebo adorned with a twisting stone path meandering through the moss and pastel flowers. I became more inspired with each click. Moulin du Roc unlocked the creativity that I had not been able to access in Los Angeles. The hotel and its gardens were a true find for me.

Maryse and Alain would use my footage from that weekend for their new brochure in the days to come. I was also hired by *Wine Spectator* to cover the hotel, and my photos were also used in the hardcover publication *Hospitalité dans le sud de la France*, highlighting Moulin de Roc. The owners and I worked out a barter system, room and board for photography. The family portrait series with their son Victor and Alain's parents was by far the funniest photo shoot at Moulin du Roc.

One of my favorite things to photograph was Alain's divine creations. Like the sherbet dessert with a sugar/honey laced basket covering on a plate delicately draped with crème citron, or the duckling breast, sliced with artistry, doused with perfumed oils, shallots, and herbs over ratatouille. The romantic attention to detail that Maryse bestowed on the gilded salon and whimsical dining rooms was so enticing that I could not stop shooting. The wine cellar, set in the underpinnings of the ancient Moulin, was a secret gem. We staged some candelabras, as the light was dim, and the effect was perfect to highlight the impressive collection of local and imported vintages collected by the Gardillou family for generations.

We regrettably said our goodbyes to Maryse and Alain and headed for our next destination, a rental house on the banks of the Dordogne River in Allas-sur-Dordogne. We wanted to see what it was like to actually live in a house, to cook, and shop at the local *marchés*. We walked down to the river's edge where we found a romantic couple of swans on their own private island, the only other occupant being a lone tree whose reflection made for some nice black and white shots I developed weeks later. Bill and I felt simpatico with the two love birds. France had become our own private island, a life raft away from the stress and intensity of our life in America.

During this week, Bill's idea of living in France took firm hold in his heart and he began his campaign to convince me that it was my path as well. I was drawn to France, but moving there seemed dauntingly incomprehensible to me. My father's pragmatism had a strong hold on my personality, apparently. With tears in his eyes, Bill asked me to give him the opportunity to fulfill a dream that he had always had of living in Europe, a writer's haven for inspiration, away from the Hollywood negativity, the craziness of the traffic, the smog, the whole scene that is LA, LaLaLand. How could I say no?

On our next trip, we discovered the café. This is when his dream started to really scare me. An old café . . . A ruin . . . The practical Virgo was fighting the Sagittarian dreamer. The filmmaker/photographer in me was mesmerized by the beautiful stone arched façade, green peeling paint, broken panes, light streaming through the burned-out shell. There was a romanticism about it all and we found out that the café and two houses could be bought for next to nothing. It seemed inconceivable. Bill began to get excited the more he thought about the possibilities. I began to get anxious the more I thought about the possibilities.

Over a bottle of wine, we talked about how cool it would be to have an indoor/outdoor café. A wine bar without a ceiling, open to the millions of stars in the clear Dordogne sky. The local ladies grew very excited at the thought of us bringing life back to their town, life which was taken from them when the café was burned in a fire fifteen years previously.

We had all kinds of dreams for the café: art, music, laughter. However, Yanette, the wonderful lady who had first told us the property was for sale and owned the *cave* in the neighboring hub of Saint Cyprien, wasn't sure it was a good idea. Daniel, her husband, told us that it wouldn't be a good place for a café or commerce as it was off the beaten path. Bill, however, wasn't ready to give up.

"Yes, but it will be so close to Saint Cyprien, which gets a huge tourist trade. Word of mouth will spread. There will be nothing like it in the Dordogne," said Bill.

I wasn't convinced. Off the beaten path? The main highway was maybe two miles away. In LA standards, that's around the block. But in the Dordogne? Sometimes dreamers just have to stick to their guns and tough it out.

We came back the next fall to get to the bottom of the reality of the dream of owning a café in France. After speaking with a British contractor, we were stunned at the price tag for renovation. Yes, you could buy property cheaply in the Dordogne, but renovation was another matter. We would soon learn, all too well, the mire of renovating a home. We began to realize that if we were to take on the project, we would need a house to live in.

Okay, it all seemed a little fishy: there was an ad on the internet advertising Villa Page, but no ad in the window of the realty company or in any of their advertisements. As we drove up to the house with the real estate agent, we were told not to act like prospective buyers. See what I mean? Fishy! And who were we supposed to be, me with my camera snapping photos here and there of our perspective new home –tourists?

The brother-in-law was helping the owners put up a new ceiling, a little "cosmetic work." Or, as it turned out, a little devious game of *"cache-cache"* to hide the defects. Much later in the *notaire's* office, when we signed the papers, we found out that the brother-in-law was some kind of engineer and rewired the electricity in the whole house, which would later become a bone of contention regarding the sale of the home.

The real estate agent was from Paris and charmingly sly. His English was passable enough so that we foolishly didn't get another agent to represent us. I wanted to see other houses, comps, although I could tell Bill had his heart set on Villa Page. So, of course, the agent took us to more expensive, inappropriate homes.

We went back to Villa Page as often as we could in the few short days we had to make a decision. It was hard to really see much, as the home was crammed full of furniture and clothes. (No closets, don't forget we are in France!) But there were three fireplaces, which they explained were definitely working fireplaces. After looking up and down over the whole house, we ascertained that two of the chimneys went nowhere. Oh really? They had no idea? What did they think we were, a couple of naïve Americans? Apparently so. We were just what they were looking for!

I must admit that the house had a dreamy charm, with the golden stone exterior, tiled and pitched roof lines, and balconies on each of the

French windows with incredible wrought iron. You could miniaturize it down to a charming doll house. The red tiled roof with scalloped tile borders formed two charming A-lines on top of the house. And the property, over two *hectares*, more than five acres, included part of a private island, which I visited often the first few years. One of the most stunning parts of the exterior is the balustrade-adorned stone terrace overlooking the river. From there, a path leads down to the river with ancient stone steps carved into the cliff for the hunters who inhabited the *relais de chasse,* a hunting lodge, a century before.

The house also came with three rental units, which would give us a place to live while we did the "minor" repairs to the house. The rental units, the *gîtes,* would also provide us with a source of income and, a pain in the ass, as it later turned out.

Bill had found his second dream home and was ready to sign the papers. This was all happening way too fast *pour moi!* In Los Angeles, before buying a house you went to at least five open houses, compared the comps, checked out the schools, the neighborhood. We were about to buy a home in a foreign country in a week's time. I didn't want to face the fact that this dream of living in France was becoming an overwhelming reality. Soon there would be no turning back. Oh shit! Why had I said yes?

We only had one week to look at other houses, make a decision, get an inspection, and put in an offer. Do you feel sometimes that you are in a vortex and events are propelling you quicker than you have time to react? That is how I felt. But if I'd had time to stop and reflect if this was the right step—what about this, and that, and the other thing—my usual discourse of Virgo logic, we would never have had this incredible experience. We would have moved to Ashland or even worse, "The Valley!" That is, the San Fernando Valley, for those of you who are not Los Angeles residents.

─┤ HIS STORY ├─

CHAPITRE CINQ

"You are married, *oui?*" asked Mme. Rouland at the bank in Sarlat.
"*Oui.*"
"Do you have with you a marriage . . . contract?"
"A contract?" I asked.
"We have a marriage *certificat*," my wife volunteered.
"Yes, but your contract, we need to see your contract."
"Oh," I said, "you mean our prenuptial agreement?"
"Yes," smiled Mme. Rouland.
"We don't have one."
Mme. Rouland was stunned by this response and looked at my wife. "*Non?*"
"No."
"We don't need one," I replied.
"*Non?*"
"We are in love. *Toujour amour.*"
Mme. Rouland smiled, but a love that lasts forever was not going to be enough. "Can you get a contract that says you do not have a contract?"
A contract that says we do not have a contract? That shouldn't be too hard. We left Credit Agricole with a short list of things required by the bank to secure a mortgage and headed for our *notaire's* office in nearby Meyrals. We had met with him once earlier to discuss the purchase of the café. Now we had come regarding a home. One of the things Mme.

Rouland had requested was a letter from our *notaire* stating that the home was worth the purchase price. He found this request quite amusing.

"Who is to say what something is worth, *Monsieur* Royce?" he said with a laugh. "To you it may very well be worth that price, to someone else, perhaps not." With that, he crumpled up the request and tossed it in the trash. If I didn't know the power of the *notaire* before, I was beginning to understand it now. He was in complete control of everything. In fact, when I questioned him once on some legal matter, he informed me in his deep, baritone voice, "*Monsieur* Royce, in France, I *am* the law." This, of course, is a slight exaggeration, but only slight.

It was at this moment that the notion of a home inspection was raised. The *notaire* informed us that this might be difficult, as it was not a common practice in France. Fine, it was with us, and furthermore, we would not buy a home in France or anywhere else that was not inspected. Our *notaire* had the solution. He dialed a number, spoke to someone in hurried French, describing me—mentioning those damn graying temples—and the location of the home in question. Jean-Pierre was a highly qualified *architecte* who would meet us there tomorrow at noon to inspect the home.

Not knowing that I would actually find a home that I'd want to purchase, along with the café, I had only rented the home in Enveaux for two weeks. The last few days would be spent at our favorite hotel, Moulin du Roc, some distance away in Périgord Vert. Each day we would commute back to the Sarlat area to explore the beautiful Renaissance town and sneak a peek at Villa Page. The following day, however, we asked a friendly maid at the hotel if there might be a shorter route. She was only too happy to give us directions. Unfortunately, this was not a short-cut and we arrived for the inspection twenty minutes late.

As we pulled up, we saw our *immobilier* with M. Berteloot and a thin middle-aged man in a designer coat, wearing hand-stitched leather gloves, holding a small brown cigarette. We were introduced to Jean-Pierre and apologized for being late. As I mentioned earlier, Jean-Pierre had completed his inspection in twenty minutes and was on his way to his *déjeuner,* lunch. He informed us that the home had passed his thorough inspection and that his sacred stamp would be on that report.

Everyone walked off, leaving us standing there, wondering what in the world we were doing. In our right minds, we wouldn't buy a home in the United States in a week with no real inspection. But here we were, thousands of miles away, in a country where we could barely speak the language, trying to buy a two-hundred-year-old stone home in serious need of restoration. We, too, decided to get some lunch and think about what we were doing. I had grown tired of rich French food and, in a daze, I drove around Sarlat looking for something other than *foie gras* and *confit de canard*. I needed something besides liver pâté and duck cooked in its own fat.

There was the Chinese restaurant on the main road coming into Sarlat, but the food was rather bland. It was, however, a place where we had actually made friends with a local French couple, Frank and Carole. They had been extremely friendly to us as we sat at the table beside them. As it turned out, we shared the same *notaire*. We had not, as yet, seen Villa Page, but we were about to make an offer on the café. Small world, Carole had just opened a restaurant called Tri-*something*. They tried to give us directions, but we were unable to find it.

As we drove around in search of lunch, I began to question everything more and more. I mean, dammit, there isn't even a good Chinese restaurant in town, let alone a Thai restaurant! What the hell are we doing?!

In France your window of opportunity for lunch closes very swiftly. Odds are, if you are not in a restaurant and seated by 1:45 P.M., you're not having lunch. At 1:50, we pulled into the parking lot of a restaurant just outside town and walked inside to find two-hour-old warming tins under heat lamps filled with odd-looking, dried-out remnants of something that might have been edible at one time or another.

Walking back to the car, we glimpsed the sign for pizza across the street. Heads hung low in defeat, we crossed the street, entered the pizza parlor and were greeted with a huge smile and out-stretched arms. It took us a minute to recognize her, but it was Carole. What were the odds that we would just happen to wander into her restaurant, Triboulet, right when we had nearly given up on the whole idea? We took it as an omen. Carole, of course, assumed we had come to see her and was delighted to see us.

We dined on salmon pizza and drank a carafe of great local red wine, our resolve restored. Or, at least, my resolve restored. My wife still had a healthy dose of fear and apprehension.

Next on Mme. Rouland's list of things required for the mortgage, was a *bilan*. For this, we would have to see an accountant. A *bilan* would show the condition of the *gîtes*, and would graphically illustrate how the *gîtes* would actually pay the mortgage. Although I was a successful writer and my wife a published travel photographer, the bank needed to know how we intended to pay our bills. Between the *bilan* and a copy of a magazine with my wife's article and photographs from our first trip to the Dordogne, the bank was satisfied. Now, all we had to do was make the offer.

On Thursday, although the *immobilier* was adamant that M. Berteloot would not accept, we made our purchase offer on Villa Page and returned to our room at Moulin du Roc to await the word. Sure enough, our offer was accepted. We would need to be in the *notaire's* office tomorrow at eleven.

That night, the owners of Moulin du Roc, Maryse and Alain, took us out to dinner to celebrate the purchase of our new home. We tried to keep up with Alain in his Porsche, but our Opel wasn't quite up to the challenge. We met in St. Jean de Cole, a quaint little village with matching blue shutters and bright-colored flowerboxes, and dined at a cozy little restaurant called the *Auberge du Coq Rouge*.

Maryse introduced us to a British estate agent dining in the restaurant and informed her of our potential purchase. Shrewdly, she asked all the right questions. We explained about the "inspection" and she was not surprised at all. I informed her that when I learned the electrical system had been installed by Mme. Berteloot's brother, I included a provision in the offer that it be inspected and approved. She then informed me that EDF would perform the inspection for free.

Friday at eleven, we were all seated in front of the jovial *notaire*. At that time, France was two months away from switching to the euro. When the sales price was converted from francs to euros, there was bit of amusement among the French to learn that the Berteloots would lose the equivalent of a dollar in the process. Everyone smiled as I stood up, reached into my pocket, and offered to make up the difference.

Everything stayed light and friendly until the provision regarding the inspection of the electrical system arose. Things immediately turned bad and headed straight for worse. Both the *notaire* and the *immobilier* seemed to freeze when I mentioned I had spoken to another *immobilier* who informed me EDF would inspect it for free. Oh? Had I hired this *immobilier* to represent me? They seemed quite relieved to learn that I had not, for whatever moronic reason, employed her.

The *notaire* informed us that yes, technically, EDF would inspect it, but they would never pass it. Why should they, he asked me. Because it is up to code, I mused. No, both he and the *immobilier* informed me, EDF would not approve it, even if it were up to code.

I looked at the clock on the wall, we still had a seven-hour drive to Paris and it felt as though we had just hit a brick wall. The Berteloots were not about to drop the price any further and the electrical system was clearly not going to pass inspection. Ah, but the clever English-speaking *immobilier* has the solution. His friend, he informs us, is an electrician. M. Berteloot and his *beau-frère* are almost finished, they have only one more plug to rewire. He will call his friend, M. Cornu, right now.

As he stepped out of the room with his cell phone, the *notaire* proceeded to educate us on the precious stamps of the professionals. He informed us that an electrician would never put his stamp on anyone else's work. Just then the door opened and the *immobilier* proclaimed that for roughly two-hundred-euro, M. Cornu will finish the work and put his official stamp of approval on it.

I looked back at the *notaire*. "But you just said no electrician would ever put his stamp on someone else's work."

He smiled sheepishly, threw up his arms and said, "Well, apparently I am wrong."

We signed the contract—written in French—and raced up the autoroute at 200 km an hour to get to our hotel, the elegantly stuffy Château d'Escliment, in time for dinner. As my wife sat in a relaxing pre-dinner tub, the phone rang. It was Maryse congratulating us on our new home in France. Feeling as good as we could about our new home and our new friends, we went downstairs and ordered a gourmet meal and an expensive bottle of champagne to celebrate. Unfortunately, we had made a slight miscalculation regarding our luncheon choice, a quiche to-go from a small roadside café. As the dinner was served and the shiny metal lids were removed, my wife suddenly became ill and rushed upstairs to our room, never to return. I sipped champagne for a moment until I, too, felt ill and raced to the room.

With the quiche safely behind us, we collapsed on the bed and recounted the adventure of the previous week. We had found a home, made a successful bid, and applied for a mortgage. We would soon own an idyllic spot to raise a child. Now all we needed was the child . . .

―{ HER STORY }―

~~CHAPITRE SIX~~ CHAPTER SIX

I had started looking at other ways to make a living as a writer. In the entertainment industry, there was a pervasive belief that forty-one was too old to write for television, even if we were writing for "blue hair" shows. I also realized that I didn't want to be among the female TV producers or executive producers who had a full life of working 24/7, a husband, and children. Sounds like the best of both worlds to many of you ladies out there I'm sure, and I'm counting those for whom it was okay not to see the hubby very often, maybe a lunch date or dinner on the weekend, and never make it to the dance recital or baseball game. I hated waiting this long to raise a child and I was determined to be among the women who balanced everything. So I started drawing from our many travels to Europe and elsewhere and I submitted travel stories to various magazines and newspapers. I felt positive because, according to the *Writer's Handbook*, I had an advantage over others because I was also a photographer. My first article, as fate should have it, was on the Dordogne. I covered our favorite hotels that we had visited on our first trip. In fact, the travel articles were part of what convinced the bank to give us the loan in France, as we had no jobs there.

Our home in France beckoned, but the family that would continue our journey with us was still to be determined. I was working as a photography teacher at a private middle school and the photographer I worked with recommended a Foster Care Agency that specialized in babies. Babies! I never knew that you could adopt a baby through the Foster Care System.

We began the long and sometimes tortuous process of taking classes, being fingerprinted, countless interviews and home visits, and then the wait. We got a call in early December that a baby had just been born, a baby girl, as we had requested. She was immediately fast-tracked for adoption and they would get back to us. Our hopes soared, but only to be dashed when we got a second call that there had been a mistake and the baby was not available to us. She had slipped through our fingers, or so we thought.

We researched adopting in France. The French were most welcoming but said to contact them once we had moved there. Meanwhile, we got everything ready, the nursery was painted a lovely yellow, we bought a crib and the theme was celestial, just as our hopes were pinned on the moon and the stars. Then we waited. It was kind of like working for the fire department; the phone could ring at any time. Talk about being on pins and needles!

When the call came, we thought we were ready for anything. There was a baby girl at a hospital in Long Beach who had been fast-tracked for adoption. She was waiting for us. We were ecstatic but in a state of shock. We put the carrier in the car and drove off to get our baby. I called my parents to let them know we were on our way. They were overjoyed. When we reached the hospital, we went to the maternity ward as instructed. The nurse checked the computer. The baby wasn't in maternity, she was in the Intensive Care Unit. What? Bill and I looked at each other and our hearts sank. The two of us and our baby carrier went upstairs to ICU. From the beginning, we had specified that we did not want a child with special needs; we wanted a healthy baby.

They have a ward in ICU for infants who are born with complications. The nurse greeted us with caution when we explained why we were there. "You have taken care of a child like this before?" *A child like this* resonated in our heads. What did she mean? The nurse told us to wash up and put on gloves and then we could go into the nursery.

We could see through the glass into the nursery where the babies were in their cribs. As we approached, she pointed out "our baby." Our hearts finally hit bottom as we saw the continually moving crib. The truly scary part were all the monitors connected to her crib. We watched for a moment feeling so torn and sad for this innocent child brought into the world unprepared for life. We jumped as a loud beeping started and a red light started flashing. The nurse explained that this happened from time to time. We learned that the infant had a defect in her nervous system. We decided to leave, clearly way over our heads.

We hurried out of the hospital, the carrier dangling by my side, and drove away in despair. I called my father in tears, trying to explain the devastating experience. Why had we been told she was a healthy baby girl? That evening, we received a call from the head of the hospital. She apologized. We never should have been put in that position. The infant was "healthy" in that she did not have a cold or any infectious disease. However, she was clearly a "special needs" infant.

The social worker called again the next day and asked if we were sure that we didn't want to reconsider our choice. We spent the day thinking about it, discussing it, looking inside and at each other. We didn't want to turn our backs on the baby, but we knew in our hearts that this wasn't the child meant for us.

―{ HIS STORY }―

CHAPITRE SEPT

It sounds like such a romantic adventure, doesn't it? A golden stone home on the river? Well, I thought so. Goat cheese on baguettes, fine red wine, cobblestone streets, sidewalk cafés, more red wine, castles on the horizon, gourmet meals, maybe a little champagne for a change, hiking on the *randonnées* through fields of sunflowers, kayaking down river, *crème brulée*, long, lazy days meandering through tranquil meadows, the insanity of humanity a million kilometers away . . .

"France? Why do you want to move to France?"

"Why not?" wouldn't satisfy anyone.

France is beautiful, yes, but even that didn't seem reason enough. The Dordogne could be the most beautiful spot on earth, but still no one could possibly understand how we could trade it for sunny California.

"What will you do?"

"About what?" would be even less satisfying.

As if they don't "do" everything in France. (Actually, that was a valid question. How long can one simply float along on the *joie de vie*, making each day your own, preparing meals from the fresh vegetables and herbs hand-picked from your garden, *pique-niques* on your island, exploring each little town, experiencing their *fêtes* and festivals, shopping at their open-air markets, sampling their exquisite menus, and sipping their excellent wines? I had no idea how long I would enjoy that life, but I was willing to find out.)

The truth is, no one could understand what we were doing, or why. Friends nor family. No one. At first, even Cynthia teetered back and forth between excitement and fear. It's hard to leave the known for the unknown. Even if the known isn't all that great, there's familiarity in it. It's simply easier to do nothing than it is to pack up your life in the hopes of something better.

I now look back at the flood of European immigrants who poured into the United States looking for that promise of a better life. How odd it must seem to Americans (and French) that we should think The Dream flows in the opposite direction. How could two people who worked in Hollywood, dining with movie stars, going to premieres and parties, how could they ever find happiness in the simplicity of a sleepy little village of 161 people?

While I was the executive story editor on a top-rated television show, I received a letter regarding violence on television and its possible effects on children. Believe me, I wanted to care, but at that moment I was putting the finishing touches on the script for that week's murder. Someone died in that little southern town every week for seven years. You'd think the townsfolk would get the hell out, but no.

Remember learning in your college psychology class about those rats that were crammed into a cage that was far too small? In short time, rats were stealing food, attacking, assaulting, raping, and killing other rats; the rodent equivalent of Detroit, Chicago, New York, Los Angeles, or any other major city in America. The point was, obviously, that rats and people do better with a little space. Perhaps, the study seemed to indicate, cities of seven million bring out the rodent in the best of men.

After the experiment, of course, the rats were returned to their own cages. Well, that's the difference between humans and rodents. You can prove to us with all the behavioral science in the world that living in crowded cities isn't healthy, but dammit, we stick it out. We have that one special trait that separates us from rats, the power to rationalize anything.

That letter sat buried on my desk for weeks. One day, when I was packing up my office for hiatus, I picked it up and looked at the staggering statistics. By the time the average child was nine, they had witnessed thousands of murders on television. Although our show aired at ten P.M., the re-runs ran at all hours in syndication. I did not believe violence in the media was the cause for our violent culture, but I knew it couldn't be helping, either.

"Do you have any idea how violent France was in 1640?" my sister, the history professor, asked in all seriousness.

1640? Well, no, the truth of the matter was that I didn't. I couldn't see what that had to do with raising our child there now, but—

"Montfort?—The castle Montfort?—the castle near your home? Do you know who Simon de Montfort was? He was evil. He slaughtered thousands of innocent people. And he was your neighbor!"

"Yeah, uh, maybe we should talk about this some other time?"

It was Christmas and we had been drinking wine—French wine, for my sister's favorite wine came from the Languedoc region, not far from our new home. My sister and my *beau-frère* tried their best to talk us into staying and raising our family here. France just seemed so far away. As it was, she and her husband hadn't come to Los Angeles in years. How would it be any different, really? We'd still only see her once or twice a year. One of those times, however, could be near her favorite wine region.

As we made all the preparations for our move, the *notaire* informed us that the Berteloots could not find a new home. We could not take possession until they found a new place. Did I want them to be homeless? Well, no. When did they think they could find a place? That was difficult to say, after all, it was nearly summer and every place is booked for those three months. My offer to let them rent the *gîtes* received a "*Très bizarre!*" from Mme. Berteloot.

Finally, word reached us that they had found a home in the hills above Sarlat. We needed to be in the *notaire's* office on Monday, June 21st at 2:00 P.M. to sign the final papers and receive the keys to our new home; a mere seven months after our offer was accepted.

In May, Cynthia sold her sporty red Mercedes convertible and we arranged for a shipping company to give us a bid on the furniture we would be shipping to France. One of the last remaining things on our list was to go downtown and fulfill the requirements for international adoption. Our plan was to travel to South America and bring the infant back to Villa Page. As we walked back to our car, we passed an elderly homeless woman pushing a shopping cart full of wilting flowers.

"How much for a rose?" I asked.

"One dollar," she replied with a smile.

I pulled out my wallet and looked inside to find a ten and a twenty-dollar bill. I pulled out the ten. What the hell, I thought, we have so much more than she has; we have a home in France. A home with its own name. I handed her the ten spot and her eyes began to well up with tears. If ten dollars can bring this reaction, I thought . . . I pulled out the twenty and handed that to her, as well. This sweet elderly woman was so moved that she hugged us both and offered to say a prayer for us.

"We're trying to start a family," I told her. "Maybe you could put in a good word for us?"

We walked back to our car with our wilting rose and the feeling that, perhaps, we had done a nice thing for a person in need. We came home to find a miraculous message on our answering machine. After more than a year of waiting, we were to adopt a child; she was five months old and her name was Natalie. We were ecstatic! We held each other tight, the tears flowing. There was only one small problem: The adoption would take over a year and we were moving to France next month.

―{ HER STORY }―

~~CHAPITRE HUIT~~ CHAPTER EIGHT

Finally, the real call came. In fact, the call we got five months earlier was for Natalie but there was a mix up in the system and she was not considered in the fast-track program for adoption. Natalie was in a foster home and we could see her that next weekend at the CPR training session. We sat through the class anxious, struggling to concentrate on mouth-to-mouth resuscitation instructions when all we could think about was meeting our daughter. We stepped outside and saw a fat little bundle in the hands of the foster mother. She was "Our Natalie" from the beginning. We were allowed to bring her to the house for a visit a few weeks later and in a few months when we completed the home study, she would be allowed to live with us. The process was nowhere near complete, but we were on our way.

We had a wonderful social worker who stood by us on every turn. It took perseverance and faith that Natalie was meant to be ours, which wasn't hard when she was in our home and we were the ones being sleep-deprived and changing poopy diapers.

It would take two years before the adoption was actually finalized. We were due to go to France at this point to sign the final documents to purchase the home, but Natalie could not leave the country. It wasn't easy, but it was arranged that Bill's mother and sister could take care of her.

We would be allowed to take Natalie to France but not for some months when we would introduce her to her new home and the adventure that awaited us at Villa Page. It was really difficult to leave her but we were very excited about finally being able to sleep under our own roof in France. Or at least this was the plan when we left Los Angeles.

When we saw Maryse and Alain again we got more than the customary *bisous*; we had moved to the double kisses stage, two on each side. What a treat to be so far from home and to feel that we were always welcomed at this beautiful retreat.

I was concerned that they didn't like the photography that I had done for their brochure as they had said little about it. Later, I found out that it wasn't the French way to gush. I personally think Americans like to gush at times, but who doesn't enjoy a good gush?!

When I had left the table at dinner, Alain commented to Bill how pleased they were with the photos and how he loved the depth of field of my composition. Maryse and he were thrilled to be able to use them in their new brochure. When I got back to the table, Bill carefully tried to reveal what they had said without gushing for them. It was very sweet and they just sat there smiling. I didn't realize at the time that Alain was a budding photographer himself and was to become accomplished in the coming years.

The artistry of the new brochure for Moulin du Roc was French from top to bottom. It was, in fact, a delightful box of treasures, tied with a simple bow made of twine. Inside the box, they had used my photographs in a miniature album, each photograph was delicately framed with whimsical birds, vines, and flowers. It was an amazingly appealing package and an honor to have my work presented in such fashion. A grand success for my first project in France.

We made a pit stop at the hotel as we were anxious to sign the papers and take possession of our new home! Little did we know that this would be the beginning of an adventure we had not anticipated in our wildest dreams.

—{ HIS STORY }—

CHAPITRE NEUF

I, like you, had little interest in international currencies and exchange rates. In fact, it was the furthest thing from my mind until the day we transferred the down payment to an account in France. Overnight, we lost $2,000 when it was converted into euros. I had no idea the difference between 1.16 and 1.14 could cost us so much money. Who knew anything two digits to the right of a decimal point meant anything at all?

We had wired the money and gone through with the deal, in spite of the fact that M. Cornu, the electrician, refused to complete M. Berteloot's little experiment with electricity, and would not be using his official stamp on the finished work. He would, however, send us a bill of 220 euros *not* to perform those tasks.

More importantly, little Natalie was finally in our hearts and in our home, for however long it would continue to be our home. Through the foster care system, we were informed that Natalie had been "fast-tracked" for adoption.

Meanwhile, we had to be in SW France to sign papers and take possession of the house, whatever that entailed. Although the state would not approve her because she had not taken the required thirty hours of parenting classes, my mother, who had raised three grown children, was given special permission to baby-sit Natalie while we were gone.

We booked a room at the Hotel Plaisance, just south of Sarlat and walking distance from what was soon to be, *chez nous*, our home. We introduced ourselves to the gracious owners, our new *voisins,* and they put their new neighbors in a delightful room across the street, overlooking a small brook. That night, we drifted off to sleep with the comforting thought that the next night we would be sleeping in our own home. (Of course, we didn't have a bed, but we wouldn't let that stop us.)

At 2:00 P.M., we were all seated in front of the *notaire's* desk. He looked at us over the top of his reading glasses and smiled.

"I see you had a good journey, but your money, I am afraid, did not."
"What?!"

I looked at Cynthia in shock. Where did we wire all that money?! I imagined some little old French farmer opening his bank statement, discovering all those euros in his account and deciding to buy a new tractor and a herd of cows. That, or a bottle of Chateau Margaux.

Nothing so tragic, fortunately. We had merely wired it into our own account instead of the *notaire's*. Mme. Rouland would have it there tomorrow. As for today, however, we could not have the keys. Not to the main house, anyway. When we explained our housing situation, we were allowed to spend the night in the *gîtes*. Just as well, there were beds in the *gîtes*.

When it came to the matter of M. Cornu's bill, neither the *notaire*, nor the *immobilier* seemed at all surprised to learn that I wasn't going to pay it. The fact that Jean-Pierre's bill wasn't in the dossier, did surprise me, but I wasn't looking forward to paying another bill after learning I'd be paying a sales tax on the house! For that reason, I failed to mention his, as yet unseen, inspection report with the official stamp of approval on the old and tired staircase.

After signing the papers, we asked the Berteloots if perhaps they might know someone who could manage the *gîtes*, as they were booked for the remainder of the summer. They indicated that they might be interested. We agreed to meet at the *gîtes* to discuss the proposition.

When we arrived at Villa Page, the Berteloots were in the lower unit, the door open, seated at a table with a vase of fresh-cut flowers and a crystal bowl of *bonbons* on the table. Without a word of English, they managed to convey to us that the flowers and the candy were part of their presentation to those renting the *gîtes*. They would greet each visitor and welcome them to Périgord Noir. They were willing to continue the service for a price.

Included in that price, M. Berteloot would perform some service that, for the life of us, we could not decipher.

Monsieur Berteloot became quite animated at this point. He stood up from the table and proceeded to walk around the room, his hands outstretched, as if gripping something.

"*Lapaloosa - lapaloosa,*" he seemed to be repeating, over and over.

Cynthia and I looked at each other in bewilderment, huge smiles on our faces. Even Mme. Berteloot had to laugh at the image.

"*La paloosa,*" she said, trying to clarify.

La paloosa? What could that possibly mean? The . . . what? I watched M. Berteloot, still wandering around the room, holding onto something invisible. La paloosa? L'apaloosa? Could those be reins he's holding? That's got to be it, I thought, the Appaloosa!

"No," I said. "No horses. No *chevalier.*" No horse *rider* was the closest I could come up with, but they got it.

"*Non,*" said Mme. Berteloot. "*La pelouse.*" She said something to her husband and he pantomimed trying to start a motor with a chord. Then he walked around the room humming like an engine.

"Ah, a lawnmower!"

"*Oui!*" they both exclaimed.

For a fair price, he would mow the lawn and she would manage the *gîtes*, which she, herself, had booked. *Parfait*. We had only a few more things we needed to accomplish before we could get back to our home and our baby, so far away in Los Angeles. We had to have the utilities transferred to our name, activate our phone, and take out a home insurance policy. Also on that list was buying a refrigerator, washing machine, bed, and crib.

While waiting for delivery, I began to remove the cracked plaster in the *salon* to reveal the beautiful golden stones hiding beneath. When I reached the corner of the far wall, I discovered the large building stones and the hollow of what had once been a beautiful arched window. It would be perfect for a built-in cabinet, I thought. Buoyed by my success with the far wall, I began chipping away at the front wall. One good blow revealed another hollow spot. When the plaster was removed, the original front door was revealed. To my horror, the timber over the doorway was riddled with termite holes.

Our French friends, Maryse and Alain, insisted we look in the yellow pages for a termite expert in Sarlat. I found an ad, called the number, and gave directions to Villa Page. At five-thirty, I heard the sound of a car pulling up our driveway. Cynthia opened the door as a Mercedes parked next to our rental car. She quickly shut the door and turned to me.

"It's him!"

"Who?"

"That funny little man who inspected the house."

"Jean-Pierre? What is *he* doing here?"

"I think he's the termite expert."

"You're kidding me?"

When I opened the door, Jean-Pierre was as surprised to see me as I was to see him.

"*Bonsoir*," I greeted him with a smile that said: Some inspection, pal, the house is riddled with termites!

Jean-Pierre ground out his little brown cigarette on my front step, entered, inspected the beam, and proclaimed it to be free of termites. He proceeded to examine the entire house, declaring it to be free of living termites. Yes, he'd even put his official stamp on it.

Passing through the foyer, Jean-Pierre pointed to the overhead light, which was currently nailed to a broken two-by-four, dangling from the radiator. He took out a gold designer *stylo* and pointed at the two red wires leading to the socket.

"*Dangereux*."

"Dangerous? That's dangerous?"

"*Oui*. Very dangerous," he said in English.

I stared at him in disbelief. "Now, all of the sudden you speak English?"

Jean-Pierre replaced the pen in the inner breast pocket of his suit coat and looked me in the eyes.

"Why did you buy this house?"

"Because you said it was *parfait!* Now you tell me it's *dangereux*. Why didn't you put that in your report with your precious little stamp on it?"

I quickly realized that this course of action was going to get me absolutely nowhere. Jean-Pierre was here and he seemed to be telling me something for some reason. I adopted the *Périgordin* custom of offering refreshment to those who find their way to your doorstep.

I gestured toward the rear porch. "Would you like something to drink? *Café?*"

"*Oui.* I would like something to drink," he said, "but not coffee."

"Wine?"

"*Eh, très bien.*"

Over wine on my rear porch, Jean-Pierre spun a fascinating tale. He recounted every detail of that chilly day in November. When he drove up, he saw that the *immobilier* was from a real estate agency based in Paris.

"Gangsters," he confided. He then formed a gun with his hand and said, "Boom-boom." Jean-Pierre told me he could not inspect our house. How could he? "*J'ai une petite fille.*"

Jean-Pierre had a young daughter and he was afraid for her. I refilled his glass and thought back to all the strange encounters, starting with the fact that the Berteloots had not told anyone they were selling—not even her brother, busily working away on the house. Then, there was the whole matter of the electrician putting his stamp of approval on the two red wires running to that light bulb.

When Jean-Pierre left, my wife pointed out that this funny little man had already lied to us once regarding the inspection report, how could we believe him about the real estate agency being run by gangsters? For that matter, our French friends said, how can you believe him about the termites?

Once again, I wondered what in the world we were doing. I didn't know who—if anyone—I could trust. On the drive back up to Paris, I kept mulling it over: M. Cornu, I concluded, had never said he'd use his stamp. The *notaire* had to know that, after all, he had just proclaimed that no one would. And, what's more, it was our *notaire's* friend, Jean-Pierre, who purposely did not inspect the home. It was a scam; I was sure of it.

We headed straight into the insanity that is driving in Paris and finally found a parking space close to our hotel. We checked into the Manoir

St. Germain and were escorted to our *chambre de caractère*, a room with character. The character, in this case, was a tiny attic apartment with a red frilly comforter on the bed, matching wallpaper, and a bathroom ceiling so low that I banged my head twice the first day.

The hotel was ideally located in the Latin Quarter, directly across from our favorite café, Deux Magots. Still, for that kind of money, I wanted a bathroom where I didn't have to hunch over like Quasimodo.

"But Monsieur," said the young woman at the reception desk, "it is a room of character."

"No," I corrected her, "It's a room *for* a character. A very small character. Like a mouse. It's a room for Mickey Mouse."

She was not amused. "There are many guests staying with us who would gladly trade with you."

I pointed to the phone. "Fine. Call them. Let's make the trade."

She looked at the phone. "I don't know who to call."

"Well, one of the many."

Cynthia had heard enough. She stepped in, apologized to the receptionist, and pulled me away.

"Let's just make the best of it," she said. "Let's walk down to Than and have a wonderful dinner."

Ah, Than, the best French-Vietnamese food in the world. We walked down the boulevard, arm in arm, retracing the same steps we had taken year after year, but something was different. After spending so much time in the Dordogne, Paris felt overwhelming. It felt foreign, but not in a good way. It was as though all of France had conspired to sell me a two-hundred-year-old ruin!

We crossed the boulevard and turned down a side street only to discover Than was closed! We wandered aimlessly until we found a crowded little café and ate a fine, if unmemorable meal. All we could think of now was our little six-month-old baby thousands of miles away. A baby for whom we would have to stay in Los Angeles another year, our home open to weekly inspections.

―{ HER STORY }―

~~CHAPITRE DIX~~ CHAPTER TEN

Every other Friday, as our moving date ("Ahh!") rapidly approached, we were blessed by a visit from Madame Bonbon, as Natalie christened her. Patricia, half Italian/half French, was our lifeline to making the move possible. She became far more than our tutor. Regarding Bill's comment on why we were moving to France, I will never forget her retort:

"Simplify?!" she laughed. "Is that what you think you're doing?"

Having emigrated from Marseilles herself, she knew that our path wouldn't be an easy one. The US did little to welcome her; no open arms here. "Give us your tired, your poor, but not your FRENCH!"

However, because we were coming into France on a non-working Visa, a *"titre-de-séjour,"* the French were willing to let us live in their country, but only as "visitors." Even after five years of paying *"les impôts,"* taxes, we were still visitors. It is true the taxes are about half of what you bring home, but that covers your pension and full health benefits.

Back to Madame Bonbon. Every Friday she would grace our doorstep with a bonbon for Natalie. The French are big on candy, sugar in fact. It is in everything; hard to find baby food without it. Natalie would hear the doorbell and jump up and down in her crib, chanting "Bonbon, Bonbon." It was her first French word, and a good one!

Madame Bonbon was an excellent teacher, giving us guided emphasis on the vocabulary and the tenses we would need to survive. But I could tell she was a little worried about us. Every time she threatened to kick Bill under the table, he would study a little harder and, per her instructions, believe in what he already knew. I was teacher's pet, for I had an advantage over Bill, I liked French and I liked school. I had also studied French when I was in college. I enrolled in several conversational French classes as well, which gave me some additional points with her.

With all of her—maybe five feet in stature—her pointed toed, often red shoes, skin tight pants, and colorful top, her *"ensem,"* she always arrived full of joy, reminding one of a bonbon herself. But this former soccer star from Marseilles was no one's piece of candy, otherwise she couldn't have made it as an immigrant in Los Angeles; she couldn't have kicked, goaded, encouraged, embarrassed, and often praised us out the door of our old life and into our new French adventure.

She was a clever teacher in that she understood the difficulty of her own language and helped us navigate the many tenses to make it a workable language for us. One of the tricks was instead of learning the future tense, you could say *I am going to* do something, and that made it much easier. Such as, *Je vais parler français bien un jour.* (I am going to speak French well one day.) I did not have to conjugate *"parler"* because I had added "going to" in front of it. A great trick to get by as we learned the seventeen different tenses that waited for us like landmines.

Patricia joined us for a dinner party with close friends and the conversation that evening still echoes in my head. It was a time of fear in America, a time when it seemed like everyone wanted revenge for what we had suffered on 9/11, a time when people looked for someone to blame. Well, our President found that someone, Sadam Hussein. Was Sadam responsible? I thought not. However, our friends to the last one felt that he was. They were ready to go to war; they were so certain. Bill and I argued against war with Sadam. Where was the proof that he and Bin Laden were in cahoots? It was a difficult time for us. We felt like outsiders in our own country. Some people, I'm sure, looked at us as traitors. We not only didn't want to go to war, we were leaving America. What more proof did they need?

Looking back, I am so glad that we escaped the terror alerts; was it yellow, orange, or red that day? Our daughter didn't experience this phenomenon: to wake up every day and know the color of your fear.

It was a difficult time and I wanted to escape it. France offered a refuge from our country's war on terror. Whenever we went to France, we were conscious of what had happened because of the tighter control on security while traveling. But once we had arrived, it was a sanctuary at Villa Page, a haven from Homeland Security, terror alerts, and the constant bombardment of patriotism. Flags on cars, flags everywhere; America is the best country in the world. Ra, ra, ra! Was is it? Getting away makes you open your eyes. I remember that CNN International carried a whole different story of the Gulf War while we were in Europe than was portrayed in America. I love my country but sometimes the idea that we are perfect and better than other countries is not entirely accurate. I think everyone should live in another country for a while and look back with fresh eyes. You see the good and the bad about your own country and its people.

―{ HIS STORY }―

CHAPITRE ONZE

We brought Natalie to the Dordogne for the first time when she was seven months old. Although it was July, we arrived at night and encountered a freezing rain. We opened the heavy wooden front door to find the home ice cold. Rubbing my numbing hands, I turned the knobs on the radiators in every room and waited. And waited. And waited. Nothing. As Cynthia held Natalie, struggling to keep her warm, I battled the elements, taking the huge iron key with me to unlock the *cave* and examine the heater.

I flipped the light switch, noting the two red wires running to the overhead socket, and approached what I thought to be the heater. Not being terribly mechanical, I first checked to make sure it was plugged in or turned on or whatever might actually be required to generate heat. The good news was that it was plugged in, the bad news was that it was not turned on and there was no switch that said: Me, you moron, flip me.

Rather than push the wrong button and possibly blow up the house, I decided to call M. Berteloot. Alas, he was as mechanically inclined as I was. He had hired a heating company in Sarlat to turn it off at the end of winter. He recommended I give them a call in the morning.

We, of course, could not wait for the morning, not with a baby. I had remembered seeing a portable heater in the storage room of the *gîtes*. Although a flashlight was at the top of our list, we had not made it to the store by seven, which is closing time in France. So, in the darkness, illuminated by the occasional lightning bolt, I made my way through the storm to the storage room. Sure enough, there it was, a heater. I picked it up to discover that, where the plug should be, were two bare wires. (One black and one red.)

With the use of a corkscrew and some shipping tape, I removed the plug from an old broken lamp the Berteloots had left behind and repaired the heater. With Natalie fast asleep in her crib in her warm little room, Cynthia and I dropped onto our bed in sheer exhaustion.

"Do you hear that?" asked Cynthia, after a moment.

I heard it. It was water. There was a leak somewhere in the room. A leak in the room in a house in which the *immobilier* swore had a brand-new roof. He had told us this over and over before we made our offer.

"The Berteloots, they make a lot of work."

That had become his mantra. They had put this new roof on the house and now it was leaking. Was I surprised? No. Not until I turned on the light and saw the steady stream of water pouring down the entire length of the wall. Fortunately, we were both far too exhausted to get terribly worked up about it. I drifted off that night wondering if the central heat had ever actually worked. Damn that Jean-Pierre!

The next day was warm and sunny and we forgot all about the heater. The roof, being under warranty, was quickly repaired. Although our original plan had been to do a bit of restoration, we found it nearly impossible with a baby sleeping in the house. So, instead, we explored Périgord Noir from one end to the other. From the charming hilltown village of Limieul, with its name that no two Frenchmen pronounce the same, to the enchanting pedestrian walkways of medieval Sarlat.

While wandering aimlessly down one of those walkways, we discovered, to our great surprise, a Mexican restaurant! El Chilango was small and easy to miss, but it was there and, what's more, they served excellent food. Most important, however, was that there was now a choice, something besides pizza and bland Chinese food.

We were so thrilled by our discovery that we dined there almost exclusively. We felt it was our duty to spread the word. We were determined to keep them afloat, but it was going to take the help of the community to do it. We introduced ourselves to our waitress, the co-owner as it turned out.

"Buenas noches," I said, trying desperately to exchange French for Spanish.

She smiled and introduced herself as Merry. "Like Mary, but with an 'e' and two 'r's."

She could tell by my terrible French and my equally horrible Spanish that I was an American. We introduced Merry to Natalie, and she took to her immediately. Needless to say, we got to know Merry quite well by the time we left.

When we returned the following Christmas, El Chilango was the first place we went. Well, after stopping in to see Yanette for kisses and rose liquor. Despite my neighbor, Simon de Montfort, and whatever horrific thing had happened in 1640, my sister and my *beau-frère* came to France to spend Noel with us and their new niece. They, too, became devotees of El Chilango. In fact, they befriended Merry's husband, chef and co-owner, Denis. We learned, much later, that my sister had sent seeds for tomatillos to Denis, who could not buy them locally.

After three days in the Dordogne, my sister, who was intoxicatedly eloquent in her opposition to our move, was now contemplating quitting her job at the university, selling her home, and moving to France. They both loved it. The pace, the people, the lush terrain, the great food and the even better wine, Margaux to be precise. (A case of which we are storing for them in our *cave*. Or so they think!)

"Do they have Christmas in France?" a family member had asked in all sincerity. I knew what he meant. He meant, do they have trees and lights and tinsel and ornaments? Carols, mangers, and fruit cakes? The answer is yes, except for the fruitcakes.

Our first Christmas at Villa Page was truly special, for we were now a family. We bought a living Christmas tree, made our ornaments, strung popcorn, and made a tin foil star for the top. (In America, as a requirement for foster care, we weren't even allowed to have foil in the house! Ah, but that's another story. One I'd love to have explained to me someday.)

We sat on the couch, holding Natalie, staring at our little tree and counting our blessings. We hadn't even moved to France yet, we could barely speak the language, but we had made friends. And what friends they were! The owners of our favorite four-star hotel, the owners of a pizza parlor, a liquor store, and a Mexican restaurant. We had discovered Villa Page a year earlier and here we were, celebrating Christmas with friends and family.

Winter in the Périgord was a new experience for us. We woke up one morning to find a thin frosting of snow on everything. As the main house was undergoing a grand rewiring, we shared the *gîtes* with my sister. The apartments, however, were not designed to be occupied in the colder months and, as a result, we were constantly blowing the power with our portable heaters.

As luck should have it, Villa Page was being rewired by our *voisin*, a neighbor named Alain. Although Alain spoke no English, we had been able to communicate quite successfully through a combination of pantomime, sketches, and my ever-improving French. Alain was kind enough to walk over to the *gîtes* and help his new neighbor restore the power.

My sister and her husband arrived on Christmas after a twelve-hour flight followed by a six-hour train ride from Paris to Souillac. We fed them a thick, warm soup and a shrimp and gruyere cheese crepe. The shrimp was sautéed in what I like to call *sauce de vin mauvais,* or bad wine sauce. I find that the worse the wine, the better the sauce.

After dinner, they retired to their attic apartment, turned on the heater, and we immediately lost all power. Confidently, I grabbed the flashlight and shone it on the electrical box, directly at the switch I had seen Alain flip up just the day before. The switch, however, was already up. I pulled it down and pushed it back up. Nothing. We spent a cold, but memorable Christmas night huddled close together, shivering.

The following day, Alain showed up bright and early for work. I explained the situation and Alain showed me another box, outside. This box, it appeared, belonged to EDF. With a special tool, Alain opened the box and threw the main switch to the *gîtes*. He then chastised me for not calling him last night. But it was Christmas, I pointed out, nearly midnight. Alain just shook his head. I clearly didn't get it. I was a *voisin* now. A *voisin* takes care of a *voisin*, whenever.

As we stood outside, our breath making clouds in the cold air, I suddenly thought about the heater in the *cave*. Could Alain turn it on for me? *Certainement*. With quite a bit of effort, monitoring gauges and pumping out water when the pressure rose too high, he finally got it working. I now understood why M. Berteloot had left it to someone else.

As I walked back to the *gîtes*, I saw a middle-aged man walking up the stretch of road we shared with the neighboring home. Bounding ahead of him was a large, gray dog. They were headed for the recycling bins at the top of our private drive. Although this was now our third trip to Villa Page, we had yet to meet our neighbor.

On first arrival in the Dordogne, two years earlier, I had made the mistake of smiling and waving to everyone I encountered. I soon learned that this was the wrong approach. The French don't trust anyone who is smiling, unless, of course, something funny has just transpired. For instance, there's not a Frenchman alive who would not have cracked a smile the time I stood on the ladder, reached outside to paint the shutters, lost my balance, and sent green enamel paint flying everywhere. Had you greeted him at that point, your smile would've been returned a hundredfold, for you now shared a common experience. You were both amused by that crazy *Americain*.

I watched my neighbor, determined to make the connection correctly. It was all I could do not to smile as I called out.

"*Bonjour,*" I said, arms frozen at my side.

"*Bonjour,*" he replied, with a nod and what I detected to be a slight smile.

I only saw my neighbor, Jacques, and his dog, Metam, once more before leaving that winter, but Jacques and his wife, Christiane, would soon become an integral part of our lives at Villa Page.

―{ HER STORY }―

~~CHAPITRE DOUZE~~ CHAPTER TWELVE

Flying internationally with a seven-month-old was a terrifying prospect. How would we keep her entertained? What if she didn't sleep? (Which she didn't!) I got ready for the trip by searching Google for the right books, toys, and snacks to bring along. The problem was, it took a huge carry-on for her and a huge carry-on for me. I had to take my camera on board, couldn't trust checking it. Fortunately, the baby rule paid off; she got her own bag even though we didn't have to book a ticket for her. There are some perks after all!

What an exhausting trip. Luckily, we flew Air France. The French love children, especially babies. I spent half the time in the back of the plane hanging out in the stewardess' area. We knew that Natalie had allergies to milk and soy, but didn't know that Natalie had allergies to wheat and many other things as well. She loved French bread, which kept her busy. What we didn't know was that the bread caused Natalie to have eczema and scratch, not to mention playing havoc with her digestion. So, she started scratching and couldn't sleep, which meant we couldn't sleep. We took turns catching a few winks here and there.

I'm embarrassed to admit that I was still learning about the right kind of diapers, sizes, absorbance, etc. Natalie was drinking so many fluids just to keep her busy that as soon as I put her in Bill's lap, the diaper leaked and he was christened. (I will never forget the look on his face!) At the stopover in Germany, we made a beeline for a clothing shop and bought him an extremely over-priced wardrobe.

But for us, one of the best things about flying Air France is the lovely bread and wine that flows your way. We also used the opportunity to practice our French on the airline stewardess who was a lot more forgiving than your average French person. Also, *"Je voudrais un verre de vin blanc,"* (I would like a glass of white wine) wasn't rocket science. However, I learned that the proper way to say it is: I *take* a glass of white wine, *"Je prends un verre de blanc."* No need to say "wine." Ah, such a beautiful but complex language. The more I studied, the more I felt I didn't know.

I spent a lot of time on the plane in the bathroom hanging out with Natalie, holding her as she played with the cups and danced on the counter. She spent hours playing with Bill's shoelaces; who needs toys? Walking up and down the aisles, playing with the people behind us as they cooed and ahh'd at her, some thirteen hours later we arrived in France.

It was always an adventure; this time when we got there it was cold in the house and naturally we had no idea how to turn on the heater. We also had a companion, a cat that was lurking around the property. We had to leave our faithful dog, Spatz, in America as traveling with an animal to France wasn't the easiest thing to achieve. Primarily because they do not have rabies, so restrictions are complicated.

I soon realized that the cat belonged to the Berteloots, the former owners. It was persistently friendly and insisted on hanging around meowing for attention. It kept trying to run into the house every chance it got. Finally, I trapped it under the sink and called Madame Berteloot to come retrieve their family pet. She didn't seem too interested but was cajoled into coming. *"J'arrive,"* she said as she hung up. This was a new expression for me. I am arriving. I arrive. I wasn't too sure, but hoped that meant she would be coming soon as the cat had gotten extremely annoying.

Bill asked, "Well, what did she say?"

"I think she said she is coming."

This was a conversation that was to be repeated many, many times over the next six years, as I would often think I understood something, but, in fact, did not.

Sure enough, in about an hour Madame Berteloot showed up. After an impressive struggle, she managed to get the cat into a box and make her way to the car, only to have it jump from the box and take off. That would be the end of that, no matter how many phone calls I tried. I'm convinced that this same cat lived on and off our property for the next several years, mostly because our dog was constantly chasing something away. Several years later, the same cat left us a little present on the back porch, four stripped *"sauvage"* kittens. It sounds awful to say *sauvage,* but in French that just means wild or feral.

We returned later that year for our first Christmas. As we drove through the chilly landscape, we were charmed by the little towns sparkling with lovely art deco lights from every light post and in every square. They reminded me of driving through Tennessee at night when I was a little girl; going from the pitch black of the countryside to the quaint little towns and their Christmas sparkles. I must admit that France out-did those southern rural spots with their artistic displays. Truly a welcoming and beautiful experience. Sarlat, one of the larger towns, was no exception and strung gorgeous lights from top to bottom well into late January. The French obviously didn't believe in the bad luck deadline of taking down the tree and lights the week after New Year.

Our visit this time would be quite different as we took up residence in the *gîtes,* our rental units; the largest of them was more like a townhouse. We were so lucky to have the rental units and over the next few years found out just how lucky. They had not been updated and there was no central heat in the largest unit, only a fireplace, which smoked unless you created a lovely draft. Kind of defeats the purpose, doesn't it?

Bill's sister, Jac, and brother-in-law, Mike, came to spend Christmas with us and the addition of two other people to keep warm proved a bit challenging, but we worked it out. Thank goodness for that smoky fireplace.

―{ HIS STORY }―

CHAPITRE TRIEZE

The more time we spent in France, the less we felt "at home" in Los Angeles. Because we had yet to move into Villa Page, we didn't feel as though we belonged in the Dordogne, either. We found ourselves between countries, with the unique perspective that allowed us to be objective. There were aspects of each culture that we came to appreciate. As someone who walks around with an ever-present smile, I would prefer a society of smilers. It has been very difficult to suppress.

Then there's the whole matter of what Europeans call *queuing*. I'd translate this into English for you, if there was a literal translation. The closest one can come up with is: waiting in line. However, the French, like most of us in the New World, don't like to wait in lines. So, half of them don't. They see it as a small revolution. Anarchy. Defying the system. These people consider themselves rebels. They are the modern equivalent of the Resistance. And, just like that brave movement, there are French people in that very line who secretly commend and support their rebel brethren. They, too, if they had the guts, would jump that line.

"*Nous sommes avec vous de tout coeur!*" We are with you with all our heart!

One day at the bank in Sarlat, I tried to introduce a new concept to the French. Normally, there are two tellers, a queue in front of each. This particular day, as it happened, there were two tellers and no line. I walked into the lobby, approached the tellers, and stood between them, waiting for the first window to open. Although they said nothing, both tellers glanced up at me. That crazy *Americain*, they must've thought, why is he standing there? No one has ever stood there.

After a moment, a young French woman entered the bank and approached. She shot a look at me, not standing in front of either teller, and created another line directly in front of the young female teller. Remembering not to smile, I explained the benefits of this new queuing system. It's revolutionary, I told her, trying to appeal to her rebel spirit. We form one line. Then, as each window becomes available, the line moves.

The concept made absolutely no sense to her.

D'accord, I continued, what if my transaction will take a long time. The person in line behind me will have to wait. The other window may open up ten times, still, he'd have to wait.

At this point, another customer entered, looked at the two of us, and stood in front of the male teller. There I was standing between the two ladies, looking, yet again, like a fish out of water.

So, yes, there are things I prefer about *les états unis*. But that winter, as we rode in the taxi from the airport to our home in the hills above Hollywood, I felt so disconnected. Los Angeles now looked like the foreign land. As the taxi pulled onto the mass of freeway exchanges, I glanced out the window at the columns of cement supporting them. My heart sank when I saw a homeless person walking to his cardboard home under a freeway onramp.

I had lived in Los Angeles for twenty years. I had taken part in a living experiment, trying to replicate the findings of that famous rat study. Every day, Los Angeles was confirming its findings and every day the inhabitants rose above the level of rats, rationalizing their existence there. I prided myself in being among the best. I had the ability to see the best in every situation, ignoring the worst. Now, however, I couldn't ignore the homeless people on the street. I couldn't ignore the trash or the graffiti. I couldn't help but compare the world I was in from the one I had just left behind.

The taxi driver inched through downtown, pulled onto the Hollywood Freeway, cutting-off the car trying to merge in front of him, resulting in a honk and a finger. Ah, Los Angeles.

We returned home to a fresh round of interviews with social workers, home inspections, car inspections, mandatory physicals, and another thirty hours of parenting classes, only offered once, at night, during the NBA play-offs.

When we arrived at Villa Page that spring, we were amazed to discover the home surrounded by flowers. We had never seen our home, or the Dordogne, in that magical time of the year. Everything seemed to be blooming—even *la pelouse*. The lawn itself was a sea of wildflowers. It was truly stunning.

Although we had a bed and a crib in the main house, the *gîtes* were fully furnished, so we took up residence in the largest apartment. This being Natalie's third trip to Europe, she was now an experienced world traveler. We, on the other hand, were exhausted. I was asleep long before my head hit the pillow.

I awoke in total darkness, the heavy wooden shutters blocking out the light, to what sounded like a megaphone in my front yard. I stumbled downstairs to discover that our *gîtes* had a front row view of a marathon. Colorful runners representing numerous countries were steadily passing by the front window. From somewhere in the distance, a muffled voice was excitedly announcing something unintelligible. We sat with our *café*—Natalie with her apple juice—and watched the show. Spectators and family members had taken up residence under our trees, their elaborate *pique-niques* spread out before them, the wine flowing freely.

We had come that spring in hopes of starting the renovation of the villa. The cracked plaster and ceilings in all the rooms would have to be replaced or repaired. Fortunately, we could stay in the apartment for now, but they were rented for the summer months. The British contractor had informed us over a year earlier, standing in the ruin of that café, that there simply were not enough workers to keep up with the demand. Jobs were booked six months in advance. Anybody worth their wages would not be available. However, as fate should have it, her plasterer could start the job right now.

Shouldn't this have struck me as a bit too good to be true, you ask? Ah, but you have the benefit of hindsight. You already know about the *immobilier*, the *notaire*, and Jean-Pierre. If you're starting to see a pattern here, then you're paying attention. I, on the other hand, was tired of looking at cracked walls, warped hardwood floors, broken windows, and the old and tired staircase. I was anxious to begin *la grande rénovation*.

Bright and early the next day, Frédérique and his assistant, Christophe, arrived for work. Frédérique was a handsome young Frenchman from the town of Siorac-en-Périgord, who prided himself on his English. While we would try to practice our French, he would insist on answering in English.

In two days, Frédérique and Christophe plastered all four walls and suspended a new ceiling in Natalie's nursery. In a week, it would be ready for me to prime and paint. Although the selection was limited in and around Sarlat, we finally found the perfect colors for a little girl's room.

Now that M. Berteloot would no longer be mowing *la pelouse*, I realized that I would need to buy a mower. I had seen my neighbor, Jacques, mowing the stretch of grass that grew along the road we shared, his dog, Metam, bounding around him. The day before, I had been on the porch and, through the trees, I saw Jacques in his rear yard, a long meadow dropping down to the river at a sharp incline. He was trimming the entire field with a weed-whacker.

Bravely, but forgetting my dictionary, I ventured next door in hopes of a recommendation for a good French lawnmower to cut our considerable yard. Reaching the end of the road and entering my neighbor's property, I was faced by an unexpected dilemma: where was the front door? I looked, for the first time, at the beautiful golden stone home with its dormer windows and natural wood shutters. The gravel road led to a garage, in which was parked a silver Mercedes. To the right of the garage was a flight of stairs, bending out of view. The front door might have been around that side, but there was no walkway or stepping stones in the grass, nothing to lead one in the right direction.

I timidly approached the open garage and called out, *"Bonjour?"*

A moment later, Metam came charging around the corner, jumping up to greet me. He was followed by a smiling Jacques. We made our formal introductions and he welcomed me to his little village. Was Villa Page to be a rental home? No, I assured him. Our summer home? No, he was surprised to learn, it would be our home, *chez nous*.

"Tout le temps?"

Yes, all the time. Once the adoption was final and we had sold our home in Los Angeles. After a few minutes listening to my French, Jacques was relieved to learn I was studying with a professor in America.

"Le Français est très difficile," he said, his intent, I suppose, to encourage me.

Yes, French was difficult. It was frustrating, and even humiliating at times. But when it worked, when I found myself deep in conversation with someone, conversing solely in French, it was exhilarating. So far, the French people that we had befriended were patient and quite helpful with our pronunciations and conjugations. Jacques, as it turned out, was no different.

Due to my lack of conversational French, the topic quickly turned to the lawnmower. Jacques proudly displayed his machine. It had a Briggs & Stratton engine, he informed me. It was very strong. Jacques picked up rocks and sticks to demonstrate its amazing abilities.

Stringing together a few sentences, starting and stopping, backing and filling, I thought I had asked Jacques where I could purchase just such a machine. Instead, I left pushing his lawnmower home.

When I returned the lawnmower, I was hot, sweaty, and exhausted from the unexpected mowing. Although I had numerous other projects scheduled for that day, I felt compelled to take advantage of my neighbor's generosity. I was a *voisin*, I had a need, and Jacques was right there to fill it.

I thanked Jacques, extending my filthy hand to shake, and tried to back away.

"Voulez-vous une boisson? Bière?"

Since we had arrived that spring, we had spent most of our time with the British contractor and her English friends. For that reason, my French had barely progressed from the previous trip. Our new British friends had warned us that the French would be very slow to warm to us. Don't take it personal, they assured us, it will be a long time before they invite you for coffee or tea. Here it was, our second meeting, and Jacques was inviting me to stay for a beer. How could I refuse?

Metam led me and Jacques around to the far side of the home, to a small, covered dining area just off the kitchen. Jacques returned with a tray of crackers, several kinds of cheese, and two beers.

I stood up, beer in hand, and admired the craftsmanship in the woodwork of his porch.

"Mon ami," he confided, *"il est retraité même moi. Savez-vous retraité?"*

The word *retraité* had never come up in my classes or my readings. *Retraité*. Hmm, should I just pretend like I knew? I found that to be a successful tactic on numerous awkward occasions. Just nod and pretend like you know exactly what they're saying. At the end, it's usually *oui* or *non*, easily determined by the expression on their faces or the tone of their voices.

Jacques must've read these thoughts on my face and said, *"Retraité."* He then made a pillow with his two hands, laid his head on them, and snored.

Retraité, hmmm. It seems so important to Jacques that I get this. Let's see, he's snoring. He's sleeping and he's snoring. Re-, meaning something you've done before; or something you're doing again. Traité. Whatever that is, he's doing it again. Maybe, whatever traité is, he's doing it again, and he's doing it while he sleeps.

"Retraité," he repeated, enunciating each syllable distinctly. He pointed to his bare wrist, where a watch might be worn. *"Retraité."* He now found my perplexion quite humorous. With animated theatrics, he hoisted the beer to his lips. *"Retraité,"* he said with a smile.

"Ah, retired!"

"Voila!"

Jacques' friend, the carpenter who built his porch, was retired. I would learn that there was a whole network of craftsmen and tradespeople who were, officially, *retraité*. Oh, they worked constantly, but they earned what the French call *du noir*, black money. This was undeclared money, shielded from all taxes and nearly everyone participated, *retraité* or not. Even M. and Mme. Berteloot insisted we pay them black money for managing the *gîtes*, and he was a *gendarme* in Sarlat! That is, when he wasn't wandering around the room, humming like an engine.

That afternoon, sitting there drinking beer and conversing with my new *voisin*, was the highlight of my trip. I was beginning to feel more and more connected to the Dordogne and the *Périgordin* way of life.

We planned to return in June, giving ourselves two weeks to finish painting Natalie's room and our bedroom, in order to move out before the guests checked-in. Since this would be our first summer managing the *gîtes*, we had been granted permission to take Natalie out of the country for more than one month.

While we were back in America, Frédérique and Christophe would suspend a new ceiling in the beautiful salon, with its mullion arched windows and French doors, the steps leading out to the terrace, overlooking the island, the ancient city of Domme sparkling at night on the distant hilltop. Yes, this was going to be a grand room. All it needed was a new floor, new walls, a new ceiling, and a few new windows.

—{ HER STORY }—

~~CHAPITRE QUATORZE~~ CHAPTER FOURTEEN

This period felt like living in two planes of alternate realties, accentuated by speaking in two languages. Occasionally, I would dream in French. Oh, no what the hell is happening to me!? Having traveled four times in a year to our home in France, I was in a perpetual state of sleepy-awakeness. Natalie had no problem adjusting to the jet lag because she took four naps a day. I know, it sounds like I'm bragging to those mothers out there who were lucky enough to get three. But the problem was, I would no sooner put my head on the pillow and she would be awake again. As soon as I got on schedule in Los Angeles, we were going back to France. Each trip brought us a step closer to moving, a step closer to living in another culture. Each week brought us a step closer to the adoption being final so that we could actually make the move.

Was I ready? Would I ever be ready? I don't think I really thought about the future, just the other plane of the present. Back and forth, back and forth . . .

I began to make acquaintances at the market and the stores. It was a small pond and I was ready to jump in and try my luck with all those French lessons. I was a bit fearless. I would launch in and describe that I needed to buy a crib or a changing table in my earnest French. The saleslady would look at me and kind of tilt her head like a cocker spaniel. *"Je ne parle pas anglais."* I don't speak English, she would say. Oh, shoot. Guess I needed more lessons from Madam Bon Bon. But hey, I tried, and she was nice about it and I left with the crib, that's the important thing.

We had to set up camp at the *gîtes*, as the house needed some "minor repairs." The walls needed re-plastering and painting. So, naturally, we couldn't live there with a baby while the work was being done. Not to mention that we had no furniture, except for the essentials and a plastic table and chairs—and oh yes, the crib—so we went back to living in our beloved "big" *gîte*.

It was an exciting time because we had finally begun work on the house. The British contractor had brought in a plasterer to fix some of the walls and the ceiling in the living room which was cracking. It was a step toward the finish line, or so we thought.

The contractor had welcomed us into her small circle of English friends and we were invited to our first party. She had a lovely renovated home out in the country. Of course, being a contractor, it was a bit of a show place for her. We met a couple of women who would become dear friends in the upcoming years, and would find themselves in the middle of a brewing storm between their friend the "Cowboy" contractor and us.

One of the women, Katie, was an incredible artist. Bill and Katie shared a love of music, taking turns improvising on their piano after our entertaining *soirées*. In fact, she was an accomplished drummer, having performed with several bands in America. She was also a painter and would be my *entre* to a gallery showing in the near future.

In France, or in America, I was preoccupied with being a mother. I had waited a long time and at forty-one, I thought I was ready for the task. Natalie's allergies were a challenge and it took us a while to see how severe they were as she transitioned off of formula to solid foods. She ended up being allergic to a great many things. When the right combination hit her system, it was a ticking time bomb. After a long day, I would slip away to the house and enjoy one of my favorite rituals: a nice long aromatherapy bath. I had discovered these Swedish bath oils in France that were addicting and I felt deserving of a bit of indulgent relaxation.

What made the baths special is that the bathroom was a solid, wall to wall, ebony-tiled cocoon. I lit candles and slipped into the lime yellow extra-large tub, big enough for a six-foot-five person. Ahhh. I can still see the candle glow off the deco tiles and the steamed covered windows. Talk about a million miles away. I bundled up and trudged back to the *gîte*, the warm glow inside permeating my skin, millions of stars sparkling overhead and the moon so bright I didn't need a flashlight.

We were on our way. We had a contractor, workmen, and new friends in France, both French and English. I was happy; sure, we were on the right path. And, of course, we were. Just because the path was full of pitfalls . . . that's what builds character or so they say. I'm not sure I was lacking in character, but who was I to judge?

―{ HIS STORY }―

CHAPITRE QUINZE

LESSON ONE:

How <u>Not</u> to Negotiate with Your Contractor

Semantics. Never get hung up on them. If your contractor is willing to admit the newly plastered walls that cracked a month later may've been done wrong, don't insist they admit the work was bad. Not right, sure. Incorrect, of course. But bad, *jamais*!

For Natalie's fourth trip to France in less than a year, we flew into nearby Toulouse. We had read so much about the fabled rose-colored city. In the years to come, Toulouse and Bordeaux would be the two major cities we would explore. But for now, with an eighteen-month-old baby, our thoughts were on racing up the auto-route, driving as fast as our rental car would go, anxious to get to the peace and tranquility of Villa Page and the majestic Dordogne River.

Since, aside from a bed and a crib, the *gîtes* were still the only space that was furnished, we settled into our old routine in the largest apartment, *le glycine*. (The word means wisteria, but oddly enough, there wasn't a wisteria in sight.)

As soon as Natalie was asleep, I grabbed the flashlight and made the trek through the grounds to the main house. I unlocked the front door and flipped on the entry light, which was still dangling from the radiator. Now, however, a red and a black wire ran along the broken two-by-four to the illuminated bulb. I opened the door to the *salon* and turned on the light to discover a dead bird on the floor, the windows wide open!

At first, I was too stunned by the sight of the bird and chill from the windows to notice that the new ceiling had been installed at such an obvious slant as to be laughable. If it hadn't been *my* slanted ceiling and *my* two thousand euros that had paid for it, I, myself, might've laughed. Instead, I shut the windows and walked upstairs to discover that Natalie's nursery had numerous cracks in the new plaster, including one large crack that ran all the way around the room.

I recalled the first time the British contractor had seen the bedrooms. She thoroughly examined the antique plaster walls by knocking on them and listening. Solid was good, hollow was bad. The hollow areas, she informed us, would have to be filled in with plaster and sanded smooth. (She failed to mention that, as a master plasterer, Frédérique did not sand his own work. That was beneath him. That portion of the job would be left to us. Along with cleaning plaster off the carpets, windows, linoleum, sink, tub, toilette, overhead light, and radiator.)

I knocked on Natalie's newly plastered walls, just as the contractor had done only a few weeks earlier. You guessed it, the hollow spots were still hollow. Frédérique had simply applied a thin layer of plaster over the existing walls. When the air-pockets expanded in the heat, Natalie's room cracked like raku pottery.

I went downstairs and called the contractor only to discover that, not only wasn't she home, she wasn't in France. She was in England and wasn't scheduled to return until the following week. My mind began to race ahead of itself: How long had she been out of the country? Was she here to supervise the work, as her *facture* for nine hundred euros clearly stated?

I fantasized a fictional letter to an imaginary advice column for *"Cette Vieille Maison"* magazine:

Monsieur,

Should I worry about the renovation
of my home in France while I'm thousands
of miles away in another country?

Monsieur Bill

Monsieur Beeell,

Good question. Yes and no. Yes, you have good reason to worry. And, no, worrying never helped anything. Besides, why should you worry? Your contractor's in some pub in Manchester and she's not worried!

Because I had not gone into detail on the contractor's answering machine, she sent word that Frédérique would be coming to the house so that we could go over the work together. I left another message stating that it might not be such a good idea for Frédérique to come over without her. The truth was, I had nothing to say to Frédérique, nothing good anyway. He had done a terrible job, which would now have to be redone. The only reason we had agreed to let the British contractor begin work in our absence was so that we could move from the *gîtes* to our rooms in the villa.

Apparently, she had not gotten that last message, for I opened the door to find a smiling Frédérique on my doorstep, ready to practice his English.

"*Bonjour,*" I said.

"Hello," he replied. "You remember me?"

"Yes, Frédérique, I remember you." He was pleased. "You're the one who installed my slanted ceiling and cracked bedroom. How could I forget you?"

In a sudden state of confusion, Frédérique entered, took one look at the slanted ceiling and, admitting it was slanted, proceeded to tell me in his best English that the British contractor had instructed him to install it on a slant. That was his story and he was sticking to it.

I led Frédérique up the creaking staircase to Natalie's room. He examined all the cracks and looked at me as though nothing were amiss.

"Yes?" he said, defiantly.

"Yes," I replied, adamantly.

We stood there a moment, staring at each other, each waiting for the other to make the next move. For some strange reason, I had thought anyone looking at their own work, cracked and crumbling, would apologize and offer to repair it. But not Frédérique. He just stood there.

I had read enough books to know the French, prejudicially speaking, are reticent to apologize for anything. Okay, don't apologize, fine, but don't pretend my little girl's room isn't cracked. It was about at this point where I lost any sense of poise. Like the crazy *Americain* I was, I began to knock on all the hollow spots on every wall. And, as I knocked, I gave a short lesson on the proper way to repair a plaster wall. When I had finished my presentation, chunks of plaster at my feet, Frédérique agreed that I was absolutely right.

"You knew that?"

"Yes."

"Then, Frédérique, why didn't you repair it correctly?"

Again, his answer was that the British contractor had told him to repair it incorrectly. I honestly didn't know who to trust. I couldn't afford, at that point in time, to believe that my contractor, and one of the few English-speaking people we had befriended, would actually screw me. Mentally, I simply couldn't add her to the list along with that gangster of an *immobilier*, his co-conspirator the *notaire*, and their stooge, Jean-Pierre. No, it had to be Frédérique. He was going to have to be the fall-guy.

When we reached the front door, I stopped and asked him point blank, "Frédérique, what are you offering to do? Are you going to repair the work, or are you going to refund my money?" Frédérique offered to do neither.

The following week, just a few short days before we'd be living under slanted ceilings, supported by cracked walls, the contractor returned to the Dordogne. She'd only be in town a week, but she'd manage to swing by Villa Page. After the *Périgordin* ritual of refreshments on the porch, we escorted her to the *salon*. At first, she claimed not to notice the slant. Then, she offered the first of what would be many excuses.

"Yes, I can see it now," she finally admitted. "I spoke to Frédérique last night. Apparently he had no choice, as the original ceiling was on a slant."

The original ceiling, of course, had not been on a slant. It had been plaster and badly cracked, but it was level. I knew every inch of that ceiling, for I had meticulously filled each crack and sanded them smooth in the spring. That's when Frédérique and the contractor informed me the repair would never last. No, the only solution, they concluded, was to suspend a new ceiling.

"Didn't you inspect Frédérique's work?" I asked, trying to remain calm.

"Of course I inspected it," she answered defensively. "But it was a little dark."

"A little dark?"

"And I couldn't see that it was on a slant."

"You know, that's interesting, because I, too, saw it at night. But I turned on the lights."

"Uh-huh," she said.

That was it, just: Uh-huh. She felt under no compulsion to continue that avenue of discussion. I found myself in that same awkward silence that had prompted me to knock on Natalie's wall, pontificating on the properties of plaster. Instead of asking why she hadn't come back the next day when it was light, I escorted her upstairs. Along with a new ceiling in the *salon*, Frédérique was also contracted to suspend a new ceiling in the bathroom. Instead, there were several patches of fresh plaster, waiting to be sanded smooth. She had no idea a new ceiling had not been installed.

"So," I said, "I guess it was dark in here, too? Please, next time, feel free to turn on a light."

The work was horrendous, our plans to move Natalie into a finished room were shot, no one had apologized for the work, nor had they offered to repair it, but sarcasm, it turned out, was completely uncalled for.

"I don't appreciate your attitude!"

"Fine!" I shot back. "I don't appreciate your ineptitude!"

"Bill!" my wife edged in with the force of a verbal sledge hammer, "Let's move on to the nursery."

"Good idea, the nursery," I said, leading the way, "which is literally coming apart at the seams."

"And let's try to stay calm," offered Cynthia.

I flipped on the light to the nursery, illuminating the cracked walls. "You're right. Calmly, I'll ask why we needed to spend thousands of euros to suspend a new ceiling in the nursery, when the bathroom—which I think was worse—could simply be patched."

Take it from me, this is not the way to conduct yourself. Listen to your wife. She's right, once again. Stay calm. *Calme et tranquille.* After all, wasn't that why we were moving to the south of France in the first place?

The contractor left that day pondering one question: If the original ceiling was slanted, how would installing a new slanted ceiling be considered a repair? I calmly pointed out that it was like repairing a cracked window with a new cracked window. Apparently, this had made sense to her. The next day she left a message with a new excuse: Frédérique had to put the ceiling on a slant to avoid an electrical junction box over the French doors.

Sure enough, there it was. Right above the doors was a small white junction box, practically flush with the new ceiling.

"In hindsight," she said, "perhaps the box should have been moved."

Suddenly, everything made sense. Frédérique had started in the opposite corner, making his way toward his inevitable rendez-vous with disaster, the junction box. Instead of starting over at the correct height, a third of the way through the room, Frédérique began slanting the ceiling upward to avoid the junction box. Clearly, she had not supervised his work and, more than likely, hadn't even checked it. When he realized he was in trouble, why hadn't Frédérique consulted with her? It was, we concluded, because of the great expense of calling England.

What started out as a disastrous trip, however, was brightened every day by the presence of our jovial *voisin*, Jacques. Being *retraité*, Jacques made himself available to us for whatever situation might arise. Whether it was translating a message on our answering machine that someone had left in French, or helping the delivery men install our new dishwasher, Jacques was always there.

During the renovation debacle, Jacques was our only relief. When we had arrived that summer, we immediately went next door and were greeted by Jacques and Christiane with an invitation to stay for coffee, Cognac, and chocolate petit-fours. While the ladies spoke, Jacques showed me the golden stone bar-b-que he was building, then walked me around to the rear of the house and proudly displayed his tomato patch. The tomatoes were huge, red, and plentiful. I told Jacques how much I loved fresh tomatoes and that I could hardly wait to start a garden of my own.

The next morning, bright and early—11 A.M.—I was awakened by the sound of someone outside, yelling my name.

"Beeeeeeeell!" the voice called out.

I opened the shutters and looked down to see Jacques. He was standing by the rear door, a large sack in his hands. I threw on some clothes, went downstairs and invited Jacques inside. Oh no, he couldn't stay, he just wanted to give me some tomatoes from his garden. They were delicious. For the next few days, we ate BLT's, salads, and made gazpacho with his succulent tomatoes.

I went next door to thank Jacques and found him watering his magnificent crimson-flowering crepe myrtles. He was delighted to learn that, not only did I love crepe myrtles, but I had planted a young sapling in my yard at home.

Again, I awoke the next day to the call of, "Beeeeeell!"

There, in a pot beside him, was a young crepe myrtle Jacques had raised from a cutting off his own beautiful tree.

"Jacques," I said with a smile, "did I tell you how much I like your Mercedes?"

From that point on, no matter what I said, Jacques laughed. I was no longer that crazy *Americain* trying to revolutionize bank lines, I was that funny *Americain*, and I was a *voisin*. I was accepted. France was beginning to feel like home. Sure, I had been screwed by the *immobilier*, the *notaire*, Jean-Pierre, and now the British contractor and her plaster-lackeys, but I had Jacques. What more did I need? I mean, besides a new contractor?

―{ HER STORY }―

~~CHAPITRE SEIZE~~ CHAPTER SIXTEEN

Bill and I had remodeled three homes in Los Angeles and survived one horrible experience in Tennessee. You would think this would prepare you for another remodel, or flip and fluff, whatever they say in LA. So what if it was a 200-year-old villa in a small town in France? Why would that matter? Maybe the term "renovation" is the key, hmm, ya think? Not exactly a flip and fluff.

I was not pleased by the way the whole discussion with the British contractor had gone, even though she was clearly at fault by being negligent in her lack of oversight on the job, but what really mattered was that she had been our conduit into the English world in the Dordogne. We had clearly burned that bridge, and this was surely going to affect our relationship with Katie and Caroline. This probably seems like a silly thought to you. What was more important, people we hardly knew or thousands of dollars we had just flushed down the toilet? But when you are on an island, adrift, trying to fit in, to cope, if someone spoke English, and you felt a connection . . .

Luckily, I had made an error writing the French check and the contractor had returned it, asking me to redraft it. You cannot write *treize cent euros* (thirteen hundred) it is supposed to be spelled out on a French check: *mille, trois cent*. Oh, well, she never got the money. We had paid the man who had done the erroneous plaster work already, so why pay her not to supervise it correctly? It was between her and her workman. I had not actually rewritten the check as I was going to give it to her in person. *C'est la vie, oui?*

What do we do now? Jacques! We were knocking on his door once again. He came to the rescue as usual with a recommendation that changed our lives, mostly in positive ways, but not all. Jacques would dip into his arsenal and produce an artisan, someone he trusted: his cousin. This referral to Jacques' cousin would be the beginning of many future friendships and, eventually, the completion of our home. But it would be a long road, full of pitfalls, moments of joy, and many memories.

Taking on a renovation in France was probably the biggest challenge we had faced in our lives and our marriage. Yes, we had written together during those stressful days of television, arguing over dialogue, character points, and plot; we had undergone the heartache of infertility and the tumultuous ride of adoption, but would our marriage withstand renovating a home in France?

At this point, Bill and I had been together for twenty years. We met in 1984, when I came out to LA to make my fame and fortune like so many twenty-year-olds before me. I was lucky, I fell in love in less than three months. Otherwise, I surely would have returned to the comfort of my family, away from the craziness of LaLa Land. Okay, I know you ladies out there are judging me, but I was twenty-four; no connections, only one friend in Los Angeles, and had taken the big plunge, against the advice of my professors. Seriously, they had said, "Don't do it, there is too much competition. You'll never make it." So supportive, wow! Bah, humbug, what is too much competition . . . a shitload!

We met on a fluke, a crossed stars kind of fluke. We were both at a party at an abandoned brewery, but we didn't meet that night. I met his quasi (cute) friend instead and started dating him. The friend told me of a job at TFI, Tape Film Industries. When I came to LA, I thought I could easily get a job; I had worked for a radio station, a TV station in Georgia, and I had a degree, la de da! Hey, I had experience. You guessed it. It was waiting tables through school that helped me survive those first few months. I got a gig at the Palos Verdes Country Club. Not bad for a small-town girl from Georgia with no connections.

So, Bill's friend was my entrée to an interview. As I waited in the small, sterile lobby, I looked through the reception window into the bustling office and didn't realize that someone was looking back: my future husband. I like that expression, so bear with me. "Didn't you see me looking back?" I would hear that often the first few years. Well, kind of, sorta, but I was nervous.

My boss-to-be, the "B" word (you will understand shortly why I am getting vulgar, well politely vulgar) made me wait for two hours for an interview. Really, if I wasn't so naïve, I would have run skipping from the building, but then I wouldn't have met my . . . future husband. Our boss had a thing about Bill and I was the southern belle that messed up her tangled web.

Honestly, this woman was amazing; a former model, she was beautiful and powerful. She found every opportunity to corner Bill when she knew I would have to find her for an appointment or a call. I would discover them together in the back of the warehouse. He looked extremely uncomfortable and she, like the bird who swallowed the canary.

Our first date was the opening of Bill's play, but boss lady had wanted to go to the opening. What?! She accepted defeat but only if she could go the following night. What? Bill came home smelling to high heaven of her perfume because she sprayed it on his scarf. When Bill told her that he was in love with me, she said, "I know a southern tramp when I see one." She could have been a little more creative, now looking back. "Southern tramp!" Come on, give me some credit. Southern vixen? Southern heroine? Southern woman? I'll take that one. Okay, I'll admit it, I could flirt up a storm. The magnolia doesn't fall far from the branch. My mother was one of the classic southern belles, beautiful and trouble, but my Dad married her, thank God! Things could have gone South; don't you love that expression? A little ole' southern discrimination at its best.

My Mom, Hannah Pauline, or just Polly to her friends, crossed paths with Elvis, and oh Lord that would have been two tornadoes in a whole world of torment. My Mom lived around the block from Elvis and she would walk past his home on the way to school. He was often out front, working on his motorcycle, and would give her the eye. She had no interest, thank the Lord, because he was a "Greezer." Whew, dodged a bullet there.

So, anyway, Bill and I had an auspicious, star-crossed lover's kind of beginning. Would our relationship hold up? Would it survive leaving all our friends and family behind to start a new life with a baby in a foreign country? Many people would not even attempt it, but then, as I said, we had faced many challenges hand-in-hand before.

―{ HIS STORY }―

CHAPITRE DIX-SEPT

"Mars is very close," Jacques said with grave concern one afternoon over beers on our rear porch. "It hasn't been this close in a thousand years."

The previous summer we had encountered a freezing rainstorm; this summer brought the worst heat wave in recorded history. Mars? Could that be it? Could Jacques be right? I had not heard another person draw this connection, but his theory made sense to me. All I knew was it was hot.

Every morning, coffee cup in hand, I would walk over to the villa and work all day. I was determined to re-plaster, prime, and paint our bedroom before we moved in. Since it was the only room that could actually be painted, I was meticulous down to the minutest detail. The room had twelve-foot ceilings and two floor-to-ceiling windows, the largest set leading to a small balcony. Cynthia had chosen a pastel peach for the walls and a cream for the trim. Although it would be the only finished room in the house, when it was done, it was going to be spectacular.

Just as I had noticed with our electrician, Alain, I found my day revolved around the bells from nearby Domme. When they rang at noon, I'd break for lunch; when they rang at five-thirty, I'd break for a drink. Every evening, right on cue, Cynthia would bring over a drink, check my progress, and fantasize about sleeping in our own room.

I had finished the interior and was now painting green enamel on the metal shutters. I thanked Cynthia for the vodka and orange juice and set the glass on the top shelf of the ladder, next to the can of paint. I reached out, brush in hand, to cover the last remaining patch of unpainted shutter when the ladder decided to topple! In a frozen moment of time, I could see the glass, a stream of orange juice, the paint can, a wave of green paint and the ladder askew. The next moment, there was *forêt verte* paint on the *pêche au pastel* walls, broken glass, and orange juice on the hardwood floor.

Three days later, Jacques' cousin Christian would look at that very room and offer me a job as a painter at his company. If he'd only known! Christian, who had restored some of the glorious castles in the area, came to examine our slanted ceiling and suggest what could be done about the cracked plaster in the nursery. Christian brought Sylvie, a young French woman, to act as interpreter.

After thoroughly examining the nursery, Christian requested a ladder to calculate the severity of the slant in the *salon*. Before ascending the ladder, he couldn't help but snicker. I could hardly blame him. He moved the ladder to several positions, then finally came down, shaking his head. He had seen worse, he admitted, but not by a professional. Not only would the ceiling have to come down, it should never have been installed in the first place. That was his professional opinion.

Because I was a *voisin* of Jacques', Christian went beyond making a recommendation to state that Frédérique and our *maître d'oeuvre*, our contractor, had intentionally suggested the most expensive solution to the problem because they assumed I was a rich American. Somehow, I wasn't surprised. Neither was I surprised to learn that, for the same price I had paid for the slanted ceiling and the cracked bedroom, Christian could have repaired all the walls and ceilings.

The British contractor had been right about one thing, a good tradesman was booked ahead at least six months. This was the case with Christian, but he would be able to make the repairs the following spring. Fine, we thought, at least we'd be in good hands. In leaving, Sylvie, the interpreter, offered her assistance if there was anything at all we should need. Sylvie was the French teacher at a British girl's school in nearby Veyrines-de-Domme.

Cynthia, coincidentally enough, was on assignment for *Wine Spectator* magazine to photograph four of the finest restaurants in the Périgord. The first three we had dined at, including our favorite on the list, Moulin du

Roc. Also included were Le Vieux Logis in Trémolat, Moulin de l'Abbaye in Brantôme, and the Centenaire in nearby Les Eyzies. The latter village was made famous by the discovery of the skeletal remains of Cro-Magnon Man.

While Cynthia was off working, I was a full-time daddy and part-time manager of the *gîtes*. Normally, since they were self-catering units and the French wanted their cleaning deposits returned, there was little to do. That week, however, as I inspected the lower unit, I smelled a slight odor. I sprayed the room and set out a new air-freshener, but three days later, the odor had returned. The tenants hated to bother me, but was there something I could do?

I talked to Jacques who recommended the owner of a local plumbing company examine the situation. It was M. Reingot's opinion that the problem was the run-off for the *fosse septique*, the septic tank. For a nominal sum, his men would construct a new system for the run-off.

When that failed to clear the air, I concluded it must be time to drain the *fosse septique*. As a city boy, I knew absolutely nothing about the procedure, nor did I know where they were located.

"Beeell!" called Jacques. Although I had only mentioned it as a possible course of action, Jacques had made the call and a truck was there to empty the septic tanks. Natalie and I ventured out with Jacques to meet the men and search for the tanks.

The Sanitra truck was parked in front of the *gîtes,* the motor running. Behind the wheel sat a grizzled old man who had not only seen it all, he'd pumped it all. He'd obviously drained enough *fosses septiques* to fill the Atlantic Ocean. Beside him sat his assistant, a cheerful young man who seemed to have no idea what the future held in store for him. Apparently, he hadn't glanced over at the old guy driving the truck.

With Jacques as my interpreter, I explained that I had no idea where the tanks were, but that I had been assured there were two. The old guy remembered Villa Page. He had been here many years ago. He quickly found the first tank. His assistant unraveled the hose, running it through the yard to the *fosse* in the rear. Cigarette dangling from his lips, the grizzled veteran flipped the switch, the truck went into high gear, and the you-know-what began to flow. (Why the hose had to be clear escapes me.)

The men found the second tank half-way down the hillside and began draining it. As we watched them work, I mentioned to Jacques that we were paying a fortune on rental cars and had decided it was time to purchase a good, used car. He promised to let me know if he heard of anything in our price range.

Cynthia and I had only spent two nights alone together since we had brought Natalie home. So, for our anniversary, she called Sylvie for the name of a baby-sitter and we dined outside, under the trees in the gardens of Le Vieux Logis. They remembered Cynthia from the photo-shoot and treated us to *kir royales*, champagne and cassis.

The next day, we returned home from the hardware store in Sarlat to find a strange message: "Good afternoon, Mrs. Royce, this is Sylvie. I think we can help your daughter. Please call me." We were completely baffled. Help our daughter what—stop smearing potatoes in her hair?

Due to the record heat, Natalie's eczema was terrible. It was so bad that we had taken her to a doctor in nearby Cenac. Although she was on both oral and topical medicines, she scratched constantly. According to Sylvie, there was a man in a small village of St. Marcilius, not far from Cenac, who was a healer. He was eighty-four years old, was quite well known in the area, and he could see Natalie Tuesday at 10:00 A.M. We could pick Sylvie up in front of the *pâtisserie* in Cenac and she would introduce us.

If this had been Los Angeles, I would've been a tad more skeptical. But here we were in South West France, not far from Lourdes. We were in the land of mystics and saints and Black Madonnas, anything seemed possible.

We arrived in St. Marcilius and rounded the side of a beautiful golden stone church just as a little old man stepped out of a doorway across the street. We were introduced, shook hands, and he beamed that impish Dali Lama-type smile. His penetrating stare felt as though he were looking through my eyes to the depth of my being. With his old, arthritic finger, he tickled Natalie's stomach, making the French equivalent of gitchy-gitchy-goo. Scratching the entire time, Natalie studied him, not quite sure what to think.

He led us around to the side door of a little room off the main house and instructed me to lay Natalie on the couch. It's not going to work, I thought, Natalie's never going to lie here, but I was completely wrong. She was mesmerized by him. She didn't move or make a sound as he held out his hands, palms down, six inches above her, and slowly moved them up and down the length of her body. He shut his eyes very tight and muttered something in French. When he was done, Natalie suddenly burst into tears. I picked her up, carried her outside, and tried to console her. From behind a barn, we heard a rooster crow. We looked in that direction just as a cat emerged.

"Kitty," she said, smiling through her tears.

The healer instructed us to stop using all medications on Natalie immediately. To our amazement, the treatment worked. He had told us, in parting, that it would take more than one session, but for three days Natalie didn't scratch. To us, it was a minor miracle.

"Beeell!" came the familiar cry. I opened the door to find an excited Jacques. He had found a car for me. A car like his car. A Mercedes? No, his other car, a Peugeot. A good car, he assured me. With a strong engine. The owner will bring the car this evening for me to examine.

We put Natalie in her stroller and walked next door with equal parts excitement and fear. True, we had bought an entire house, but for some reason, buying a car was intimidating. We were introduced to the owner of the car, Ramon, a charming young man with a dark complexion. He told us he lived just across the river. In fact, you could see his house through the trees. I had always heard that the French took English in high school. Although Ramon was very young, he didn't speak a word of English. This struck me as odd, but I simply noted it in passing.

Everything looked fine on the Peugeot. That is, until I walked around to the passenger door and discovered the handle was missing. On closer examination, it was clear that the handle had been pried off with a crow-bar.

"*Oui*," admitted Ramon, the car was broken into.

"In Sarlat?" I asked in shock.

"*Non*," Ramon assured me.

"*Non*," echoed Jacques with a laugh.

"Toulouse."

In Toulouse, they agreed, there was crime. Not in Sarlat. No crime in Sarlat? I was tempted to tell them the story of our home purchase, but I thought better of it. I was just happy to know the car could reach Toulouse.

Ramon assured me he would repair everything. Jacques told me I had nothing to worry about. The car would be thoroughly inspected by the *Contrôle Technique*. Before the car could be sold, everything would have to be repaired.

The following week, with assurances from Jacques that 3,750 euro was a fair price, we took possession of a ten-year-old Peugeot. That night, we discovered that the brake lights and turn signals didn't function when the headlights were on high beam. We called the number Ramon had given us, only to learn that he was out of town. He was on vacation. Hmmm, I hmmed. Yesterday we gave him the equivalent of $4,000, and now he was gone.

After all we'd been through, I started contemplating that Peugeot sitting out there in our driveway. The one that had been broken into and possibly stolen in the big city of Toulouse, 90 km away. When had it been broken into, I wondered? How long had Ramon been driving it around that way? After all, there was a baby's seat in the rear behind the passenger door, a door that couldn't be opened. Yes, I concluded, the break-in had to be recent.

What were the odds? I told Jacques I was looking for a used car, a French make, for three to four thousand euro. Two days later I'm summoned with a "Beeell!" and introduced to Ramon who is selling a French car in my price range. A car that was recently broken into. Oh, and what did Ramon do for a living? He was a painter. Not just any kind of painter, mind you. Ramon painted cars. Cars! It was too perfect. The cars were stolen in Toulouse, brought to the Dordogne, painted, and sold to unsuspecting morons like me. I just didn't want to believe that kindly, old Jacques was the ring leader, but how else could you explain that Mercedes in his driveway? After all, the man is *retraité*.

The next day, Jacques brought over another bag of tomatoes and inquired about the car. When I told him about the wiring problem, Jacques was surprised, but assured me Ramon would fix it. Was Ramon French, I asked in passing. Yes, of course he's French. I tried to tip-toe around what might be a racially charged topic, namely the fact that Ramon was much darker than any Frenchman I had met. Ramon, I learned, was from French Morocco.

Ah, Morocco. That explained why he didn't speak a word of English. Morocco. Hmmm. He sells a potentially stolen car and disappears with a bag full of money. I very quickly convinced myself that I had unwittingly supported a terrorist network. Who would believe I had uncovered a cell right here in Périgord Noir?

I spun my wild theory to Cynthia, hoping she would shoot it full of holes. I was expecting her to laugh and say, "Ramon? You're nuts!" But no. She bought it hook, line, and sinker. Once again, we had trusted the wrong person and were screwed. Now what?

While we were standing there, looking at the Peugeot, a tenant from the *gîtes* strolled over. Naturally, we didn't breathe a word of our suspicion. She took one look at our new car and said—I kid you not—"Is it stolen?"

"Why did you say that?"

"Chimay," she said. "Look. Right here." She pointed to a decal on the rear window, proclaiming the car to be from a dealer in the little town of Chimay, just south of Paris. This was her town. She was flabbergasted to see a car from Chimay here in the Dordogne.

Cynthia and I looked at each other, too stunned to speak. This couldn't be happening! Well, maybe it wasn't. It was, after all, circumstantial evidence. We really had nothing concrete to go on. However, the entire way to Perigieux to register the car, I imagined getting pulled over by a gendarme—like M. Berteloot—and shipped off to Devil's Island.

Days passed, Ramon returned from wherever he was, apologized for any inconvenience, and fixed the wiring problem. Okay, he apologized, so maybe he wasn't exactly French, but he fixed the car with a smile. Would a terrorist do that?

The next time I saw Jacques, it wasn't preceded with the customary: "Beeell!" That was because he was in the company of his older brother, Henri. Henri had come with Jacques, his cousin, Christian, and a master carpenter named Francis, to act as interpreter regarding the formal details of the *rénovation*. Jacques, respectfully, let Henri do all the talking.

Henri had worked in the United States and his English was impeccable. We offered the gentlemen a beer or an aperitif, but as they had just come from Jacques', they had already partaken in the *Périgordin* custom. For this reason, all barriers seemed to be down. The men spoke freely about the condition of the home and the quality of the work performed. They also informed me that Villa Page had gone an entire year without a roof! Ah, that might explain the warped floors.

"Your *immobilier*, he did not tell you?"

"Uh, no, it must've slipped his mind."

In an attempt to make the cracked plaster walls feel a little more like home, I had tacked an old poster of Sarlat over the fireplace. I found the poster, depicting the town square with a woman standing next to a gaggle of geese, rolled-up on the top shelf of a closet. In one of those amazing coincidences, the men recognized the woman as their cousin! The poster was over fifty years old. Yes, their cousin was not only still alive, she was quite famous for her *foie gras,* goose liver *pâté.*

After examining the *salon*, we found ourselves upstairs in the cracked little nursery. Henri seemed genuinely concerned that we had been through so much. He assured me that I was now in good hands.

"You now will have working for you the best workers in all the Dordogne."

"Well good, Henri," I said, "Because I've had the worst!"

We ended up in the freshly painted master bedroom. Henri looked out the window and pointed at the side wall of the *gîtes*.

"Do you see there, where the stones are red?"

I had noticed that a section of the wall was a different color, but I assumed they were simply quarried from another area.

"It's from the fire."

"Fire?"

Although Henri was just a small boy at the time, he was old enough to remember World War II. The Nazis, he told me, had dropped a bomb on Villa Page.

"There were some very brave men. They were *La Résistance.*" The other men drew respectfully quiet, their heads hung low, eyes on the floor. Henri looked out the window. "From that spot, they supplied gasoline to the Resistance fighters."

I told Henri that I knew about the Resistance movement, but the truth was, most of what I knew was from Hollywood movies like *Casablanca* and *To Have and Have Not.*

"The Nazis," said Henri, almost in a whisper, "they were not good people."

Not good, Henri? With his command of the English language, Henri could have called the Nazis anything from horrific scumbags to evil personified. Instead, Henri chose to tell me a story. Turning and looking out the window to the permanent scar on the golden stone wall, Henri recounted a day in a village not far away.

"Oradour . . ."

That's all he said, but the men in the room knew the story and, once again, they would listen and bow their heads in respect.

Henri turned away from the window and looked at me. "The men were slaughtered and hung like meat in the *boucherie.* The soldiers, they gathered the women and the children—five hundred—they locked them in the church. Then, they set the church on fire."

The only sound in the room was a sniffle from Christian. Although no one cried, there were tears in everyone's eyes. I don't remember how we got out of that room and down those stairs, but I do know that I'll never be able to look at that wall the same way. I'll never again admire the reddish tones in what should have been golden stones. It made me proud to think I owned a home that was, in some small way, a part of *La Résistance.*

A home that was bombed by the Nazis, what next?!

―{ HER STORY }―

~~CHAPITRE DIX-HUIT~~ CHAPTER EIGHTEEN

While we were there in the summer, I was managing the gîtes in my pidgin French and was learning all the ins and outs of running vacation rental units. We had clients from all over the world, but mostly from France, Germany, and Australia. Few Brits wanted to stay in the *gîtes,* as they preferred more upscale lodgings.

The former owners of the *gîtes,* the Berteloots, were in the practice of welcoming the guests upon arrival and bidding them a *bon voyage* with their deposit check in their hands upon departure. After attempting this a few times and realizing that there was no way to predict when someone would arrive, I preferred the version which had been used by rental homes we visited: a key left under the mat. I didn't leave them high and dry, there was a detailed book in each unit for them to look up any questions they might have.

I always left a bottle of wine. (Thanks to our proximity to the Bordeaux region, a good bottle could be had for under six euros!) I would stop by some time the following morning, mid-day, or afternoon when it seemed appropriate to check in. Few complained of this practice. I did have one French madam who spoke perfect English and wanted me to write a full inventory of every piece of silverware, dish, and linen, so that I would not accuse her of stealing anything upon departure. Ugh! Well, at least now I had an inventory.

The departure! That was a whole 'nother thing. We held a security deposit which would cover anything broken, missing, or if they left the place without cleaning. Self-catering *gîtes* meant that they were to clean and leave the property how they found it. The crucial part here is the "how they found it." I was soon to learn how fastidious the French and Germans were about this cleaning. Everything had to be spotless, no small cobweb or speck of dust under the bed, no crumbs in the drawers or one single hair on the bathroom floor or basin. Now, I am not saying that everyone was this way, but in general I learned very quickly how to play this game. I made it clear in the contract that they would receive their deposit check a week after their departure. They signed the contract without a word of complaint, but it was a whole 'nother story when it came time to leave without their money. I had one lady run down the hill onto our property as we were leaving to find out when I would be over to inspect and another who refused to leave until I had gone over everything in the apartment with a fine-tooth comb.

I met some wonderful families and the French were by far the politest, to a fault really, because it wasn't until after they left that I would find out they needed an extra pillow or the coffee machine broke during their stay. The Dordogne was just being discovered by America, so they were trickling in. They were by far the neediest, not hesitant to shout out that they needed something or had questions. However, I appreciated their communication, letting me know right away if something didn't work.

On more than one occasion, the clients would become quite rowdy; drunk on good cheap wine, singing at the top of their lungs, or carrying on in loud voices late into the night. The nice thing was, not speaking their languages, I never knew if they were passionately discussing the weather or about to strangle each other. Sometimes ignorance truly is bliss.

—{ HIS STORY }—

CHAPITRE DIX-NEUF

Although, like the farmer that lived across the road, I worked from the moment I awoke until the five-thirty bells, I found there was always time to do the little things. Since there were no Thai restaurants, I learned to prepare several of our favorite dishes, including mint noodle with chicken. In the long, golden rays of sunset, Natalie and Cynthia would stroll down the driveway, walk up the pathway leading to the wishing well, and pick fresh mint growing wild in the flower beds.

At the noon bells, with Natalie strapped into a pack on my back, we'd venture through the woods, down the old stone stairway built into the side of the cliff, and wade across the shallow side of the river to our island. Finding a sandy beach, we'd set out our *pique-nique* and watch the parade of kayaks and canoes floating by; the sounds of happy people on vacation, the laughter, and the various languages filling the air. Once, we were even regaled by a passing Italian aria.

That summer brought all kinds of new sights and sounds. From the soothing *ba-ah-ahs* of the sheep in the meadow past Jacques' to the "kitty" that only Natalie could see. That is, until one day I was painting the rear porch and saw the "kitty" myself. The creature had four legs and a tail like a cat, the body was a bit longer and the legs a tad shorter. This particular "kitty," however, had the snout of a dog. It quickly climbed the tree, leaped to the next tree, and was gone.

Jacques came over, having just sampled the wares at a wine festival in Beynac. He brought back a brochure for a white wine he thought Cynthia would enjoy. I described the animal I had just seen to him, but Jacques had absolutely no idea what I was talking about.

He scratched his head. "*Comment-dit* . . . Ah, squirrel."

"*Non, plus grand. Comme un chat avec le visage d'un chien.*"

Like a cat with the face of a dog? Jacques just laughed and shook his head. As he was leaving, Cynthia invited Jacques and Christiane to dinner on Sunday. We had meant to invite them over as soon as we had a table and chairs, but here it was our last week and we had yet to find chairs to match our table. Jacques was so touched by the gesture that he accepted without checking.

Literally translated, *beau-père* means beautiful father. It sounds so much nicer than father-in-law, doesn't it? For our last few weeks in France, we were joined by Jim, my *beau-père*. Jim came to see our new home, spend time with his new granddaughter, and help us paint the shutters.

Dinner that Sunday night was a real experience for Jim, as well as for us! We had decided to use Jacques' tomatoes in each course. For the *hors d'oeuvres*, I made a dough and formed it into miniature pizzas, covered them with sundried tomato pesto, topped with a slice of tomato, sprinkled with gruyere cheese, and baked on the *brioche* setting. Next on the menu would be a mixed green salad with walnut oil bought fresh at the market in Sarlat with, of course, Jacques' tomatoes. Followed by homemade spaghetti and real French bread.

Jacques and Christiane arrived right on time, a bottle of champagne and a bottle of red Bordeaux in hand. For the first time, we were greeted with kisses and invited to use the informal "*tu*" when addressing them. Now, you may not know this, but "*tu*-ing" someone is huge in France. None of our French friends had, as yet, invited us to "*tu*" them. Even Yanette, who was quick with the kisses, still used the formal "*vous*" when addressing us. Although we were honored by the gesture, we had not anticipated it coming quite so quickly and hadn't practiced the conjugations for *tu!* (Thank you very much, unfortunately, we have no idea how to *tu* you.)

Back in Los Angeles, I had searched my extensive CD collection for any song that mentioned France, from Sinatra singing "April in Paris" to the Beatles' "Michele." As everyone headed out to the rear porch and the plastic patio furniture we borrowed from the *gîtes*, I turned on the music. With Frank singing about April, chestnuts in blossom, and holiday tables under trees, I put the appetizers in the oven, opened the champagne, and got the glasses.

I stepped onto the porch as Dino began *La Vie en Rose*. Jacques smiled, looked at me and said, "The mouse pack."

After a moment of confusion, followed by a good laugh, my *beau-père* informed him that it was the Rat Pack. Jacques thanked Jim for the correction, but was clearly baffled.

"The rat," he said, "it is a good thing?"

Uh, no. Calling someone a rat was not a compliment. They could've called Frank, Dean, and Sammy a pack of anything, why they chose rats, I was at a loss to explain. Instead, I raised a glass of champagne and made a toast. "*A nos nouveaux amis et voisins*." To our new friends and neighbors.

Jacques was touched by the toast and honored to learn his tomatoes would be the centerpiece of the meal. Course after course, the wine flowed as freely as the conversation—almost entirely in French. Christiane and Jacques had grown up just a few kilometers from each other, not far from where they now live. For hundreds of years, their families were born and raised here. Now, however, their children could not afford to stay. There were no jobs in the area that paid enough to afford a home in the escalating housing market. Jacques and Christiane were truly saddened by the thought that, after hundreds of years, generation after generation, their children would be forced to leave.

When the meal had finished, Christiane turned to me and asked why we were moving to France. I had never truly answered that question to anyone, but now, here it was, my own neighbor, asking me why I was leaving America. Why I was *choosing* to live thousands of miles away from the land where I was born and raised. The land of, for however brief, my ancestors. My Irish ancestors, who had come to America in search of a better life. Was it still a better life? It was busier, had more things, and was far more expensive, but was it better?

I looked across the table at my father-in-law before answering Christiane. "Our *notaire*, he said to us, 'In France, all babies are beautiful.' When he said that, Christiane, I got defensive. What is he saying? In America, all babies are not beautiful? But I now know what he meant. It's sad, but in America, my baby is beautiful, but your baby might be homeless."

Jacques and Christiane looked at me in bewilderment.

"In America, money is the most important thing. In most families, both parents work. They don't raise their own children. They work so they can buy *things*. America is about making money to buy things. And we've got great things to buy. We'd rather pay thousands of dollars for those great things than pay attention to our children."

I finally managed to look at my *beau-père*. Although he appeared to agree with what I was saying, I think he was more than a little surprised to hear these words coming out of me.

"I am not a capitalist," I continued, "I care about my *voisin*." When I chose that word, I almost cried. "I think it is wrong to have billions of dollars while children in America are homeless and dying of starvation. Fifty thousand homeless children . . . I cannot live in a country that chooses to bomb other countries instead of feeding its own children. I prefer to live in a country where all babies are beautiful."

I didn't mean to make my guests cry the first time they came to dinner, I promise you. It was, perhaps, that last glass of wine, but whatever it was, I had said it. And the response, the tears from Christiane, proved to me that our *notaire* was correct. I had chosen the right people and the right land in which to raise my child. These were the values I wanted to permeate through her being. I wanted Natalie to share what we experienced that first night in Domme; that we were exactly where we were supposed to be. Where the people, as Guy Weir said, had a reverence for the land and for their ancestors. In the spirit of my own ancestors, I would struggle to find a new land of opportunity for my children. A land of new hopes and dreams. Where every child is beautiful.

The hour got late, we shared a sip of Armagnac and kissed *bon nuit*. In parting, having recently finished his stone bar-b-que, Jacques invited us to dinner on Wednesday night. The same thought ran through our minds: Wow, this is so cool! Our first invitation into someone's home for dinner!

But we're going to Moulin du Roc Wednesday to see Maryse and Alain and eat a four-course meal and won't be able to eat for two days . . .

"We'd love to come. What time?"

Befittingly, the last few days in the Dordogne would be spent eating. The next night we headed for Sarlat, strapped Natalie into her stroller, and wandered through the pedestrian area, soaking it all up, as this would be our last visit to the beautiful city for quite some time.

The sun was setting and the old gas lamps were being lit as we rolled up to an outdoor table at El Chilango, sat, and watched the world go by. Merry stepped up with menus and greeted Natalie. Merry was being run ragged by a party of twelve seated at several tables beside us. They were Brits on vacation and were quite demanding. The usually unflappable Merry seemed to be flapping.

When she took our order, I thought she was tired. I had no idea it was far more serious. As she set down our meals, I noticed that Merry's eyes were red and that she was struggling to smile. This couldn't all be over a rude table of Brits.

"We are closing the restaurant," she said, her eyes filled with tears.

"No." I couldn't believe it. I felt almost as bad as Merry. El Chilango was one of the things that was going to make the transition a little easier. I was devastated. Afraid she would burst into tears, Merry quickly retreated. Cynthia and I looked at each other in shock. Not only did we love the little restaurant, we had come to feel as though Merry was our friend. She was a smiling, friendly face that was always happy to see us.

We tried to enjoy our last meal on our last night in Sarlat, but we couldn't eat. When things slowed down, Merry came back to our table. She had no idea what they would do, but they would not be opening another restaurant. Denis, her husband and chef, was also a gourmet vegetarian chef. Nearly half of the British population, as it turns out, is vegetarian. Cynthia got an idea. Sylvie, she told her, is the French teacher at a British girls' school. Maybe she could help. She told Merry we would contact Sylvie and give Denis a glowing recommendation.

When we'd finished our meal, Natalie, nineteen months old, walked over to Merry, patted her and said, "Ohhhhh," as though she knew Merry needed comforting. We paid the bill, exchanged phone numbers, and made a deal: We'd cook Thai food for them if they'd cook Mexican food for us. We shook on it.

Lunch at Moulin du Roc was everything we knew it would be. After a bottle of wine and a long ride home, we were exhausted, not to mention stuffed. With Natalie asleep in her crib, we stretched out on our bed. A few minutes later, we were awoken by the sound of thunder. It was pouring down rain.

With umbrellas in hand, we ventured next door to find Metam and Jacques, dressed in his usual attire: jeans, sandals and a short-sleeve pullover shirt. He was standing under an umbrella in front of his new bar-b-que. Although we were in the midst of a lightning storm, Jacques was determined to get it lit.

Christiane invited us to sit in their *salon,* a tastefully decorated room with leather furniture, a grand fireplace, hand-carved beams, and a long walnut table for Sunday feasts with the family and *grande soirées*. We made ourselves comfortable and Christiane brought out champagne and appetizers. Jacques joined us, an encyclopedia in hand. He opened the book to a page on indigenous animals and pointed to the creature Natalie and I had seen.

"Poutoir," he said.

He then went on to tell us that this animal was used in hunting rabbits. The hunter would send it into the hole to flush out the rabbit. After a short exchange with Christiane, Jacques got up and rummaged around in an antique walnut cabinet. He came back with an old black & white postcard and presented it to us. It was a photograph of Villa Page from the turn of the century. Jacques had found it hundreds of kilometers away in an antique shop in Marseilles.

Our home had been a postcard. Someone had been here, long before it was ever a tourist area, seen a postcard of Villa Page, bought it and mailed it to a friend or a loved one in Marseilles. The postcard was treasured, kept as a memento. A *souvenir*. Only to be discovered many years later by Jacques, bought, and returned to Villa Page. What were the odds?

Jacques and Metam braved the storm to check on his coals while we perused his photo album from the twenty-five years they had spent in

Senegal. Jacques had gone to Africa to erect drills, bringing water to the draught-stricken area. The photos were of a much younger and very happy Jacques and Christiane in villages with tribesmen, surrounded by goats and chickens. Four months of the year, they would return home to their friends and family in the Périgord.

Now, Christiane worked two jobs; three days a week at the pharmacy in Carsac and two days a week at the *marie*.

"You work two jobs?" Jim said, quite impressed.

"And Jacques is *retraité*?" I said with a smile as he entered. "Hardly seems fair."

Christiane grew very serious. Jacques couldn't work, she told us. It was a miracle he was even alive. Jacques had been hit by a car only a few years earlier. He wasn't expected to survive. After a month in the hospital and numerous surgeries, Jacques came home and valiantly fought back, learning how to walk all over again. It was a miracle, she said. And what was the source of this miraculous recovery? Jacques returned to the room with his treasured possession, a Black Madonna.

Christiane gestured for us to sit at the grand table, set with fresh bread and a bottle of wine. Christiane served plates with large portions of her home-made *foie gras* and Jacques poured a Sauterne from Bergerac. The combination of *foie gras* on bread, followed by Sauterne was *parfait*. Although it was excellent, Jim, Cynthia, and I were still full from lunch. After a couple of bites, we looked at each other. What were we going to do? Jacques got up to tend to his bar-b-que. I looked over at Metam, but I was too late, he was up, out the door, and into the lightning storm with Jacques.

We complimented Christiane, commenting on how rich it was, and how we wanted to save our appetite for Jacques' main course. She gathered our plates and returned with a mixed green salad garnished with duck gizzards. (There are two kinds of people in this world, those who eat animal innards, tongue, tripe, intestines, sweet breads, brains, kidneys, and livers, and those who don't.) I pride myself in not even knowing what a gizzard is, but bravely I sampled the local cuisine. Then, again, I looked for Metam.

The conversation wandered from topic to topic, from President Bush, to the school Natalie would be starting next year, to their son and his girlfriend, an accomplished dancer. They raved about her abilities and told us that, someday, she would perform "Singin' in the Rain" for us.

All evening, the conversation was sprinkled with English. Although they'd never had a chance to practice it, they had both taken English in high school, some forty-odd years ago. Jacques, however, still remembered his first lesson. With great pride he said, "My tailor is a rich man."

I looked at Jacques' casual attire and said, "Well, maybe not *your* tailor."

Jacques laughed and said, "My second lesson. My tailor is *not* a rich man."

Jacques' tailor may not have been a rich man, but Jacques, himself, was rich in ways that had nothing to do with money. Jacques had the wealth of knowing he was a *bon homme*, a good man. He was loved and respected by his entire community. He treasured every moment of life, for Jacques had been smiled upon by the Black Madonna, herself.

―{ HER STORY }―

~~CHAPITRE VINGT~~ CHAPTER TWENTY

Okay, I couldn't avoid the reality anymore: we were moving to France. The Check List on moving to another country for many begins with selling their house. Some people move so that they can live in their dream home, but we had created an oasis for ourselves at our Micheltorena home in the Moreno Highlands area of Silverlake. We bought the house when it first came on the market ten years before and scooped it up before they could hold the open house. The home hadn't been on the market in over forty years and was built as the model home by Antonio Moreno, the famed 'Latin Lover' of the silent screen. Moreno had married oil heiress Daisy Canfield and developed a section of Los Angeles that is now known as Silverlake. Rumor has it the Latin Lover designed our home for his mistress.

We had taken the money that we had made on *In the Heat of the Night* and brought the home back to its former glory with a few new touches, including a koi pond, a raised brick terrace, and a gazebo with a view of the lake. We added sconce lighting and a stunning kitchen with handmade tiles. After two years of hard work, the garden topped the Silverlake Secret Gardens Tour. It was hard to leave our home for the unknown, but as fate should have it, this was the perfect time to capitalize on our investment.

Some of you are wondering: How does one actually move to a foreign country? First, you make an appointment with the French Embassy and apply for the *Visa de long séjour*, which means long stay. Once you are there for more than a few months, you have to apply for the *carte de séjour*, which has to be renewed each year. You can only get the *Visa de long séjour* if you can prove you have the means to support yourself living there.

In order to stay in France, we would have to be examined by one of their doctors in the county seat of Perigueux to make sure that we weren't sick and wouldn't become a burden on their system. We took an HIV test and also had to have x-rays of our lungs. This process was a bit nerve-wracking before and during the exam. No, I didn't think I had HIV or anything seriously wrong, but who wants to know until they really have to?

We were required to fill out the paperwork that the goods, furniture, and clothes we were bringing into France were for our use only and not for sale. I didn't realize this also concerned my photography. *Sacre bleu!*

It was actually a lot more complicated to bring in our animals. Although France doesn't make you quarantine your dog, to get the rabies certificate you must go through a complicated process. We had our ever-faithful dog Spatz, who we had found as a stray. Carroll O'Connor was convinced the dog was pure-bred because she was so beautiful.

Well, Spatz certainly changed our lives when we found her. We were working on location in Georgia and were going to play tennis in the middle of the day during the week. (The kind of thing a writer working on location on a TV show does.) We had just picked up our usual cheese and egg biscuit from Mamie's Drive-Thru. I can taste it now. Please! No, you can't get this biscuit at McDonald's or Jack in the Box. Yes, they do have a cheese and egg biscuit, but not like this. A real biscuit like my grandmother made, with eggs and cheese cooked in butter that very morning. Mmmm. Ok, I have to say it, a little bit of heaven.

Anyway, I see this puppy running from the garbage dumpsters to hide in the large draining pipe. Probably about three months old, black and tan, with a coat like a golden retriever. As she runs, I see that one of her legs is broken. (A special needs dog.) She hid in the large drainage tube from us, but she smelled those Mamie's biscuits.

"Oh, it's a puppy," I said.

Those fateful words were the beginning of a thirteen-year-old relationship with probably the best dog either Bill or I (or most people) will ever come across.

We never got to eat those biscuits, but she did. Inch by inch, she crawled forward timidly to lick up the morsels used as bait to draw her to us. The local vet said he could fix the leg, but it would not be cheap and she would likely have problems when she got older. We had a no-pets clause on our apartment in Los Angeles and couldn't keep a dog, but someone would want her.

She was so cute in that little red cast. I got her a pillow and brought her into work with me. (I could do those things being the Executive Story Editor and the "Little Girl" to Bill's "Meathead" from Archie Bunker.) Of course, we moved from that apartment and found our home in Silverlake so that we could keep her. We named her Spatz because she had white paws like the old-time spats Fred Astaire wore.

So, I proceeded to get her tested for rabies to move to France with us. First, you have to have them tested to determine if they have rabies before you can get them inoculated. This test goes off to Houston. (I know. We live in Los Angeles, one of the biggest cities in the US, but no they couldn't do this test here.) Okay, check, no rabies. Then she has to be vaccinated and it can't be more than two weeks after the test. Stressola!

One of the things that had been difficult about going back and forth to France was leaving Spatz. Our friends took care of her, walked her, petted her, and fell in love with her. She was thirteen and had begun to falter. She grew weaker as the move grew closer. Finally, I took her to a specialist when she wouldn't eat, even if Natalie fed her out of her hand. The doctor said she had diabetes and that she should stay at the hospital to receive treatment. I will regret the rest of my life not taking her home . . . She would not be going with us on our French adventure.

Oh, Spatz. You were a good one.

―{ HIS STORY }―

CHAPITRE VINGT-ET-UN

In the Périgord, there is time to contemplate things like time. Although they have the same number of numbers on the clock, there just seems to be an abundance of time in the Dordogne. I am continually amazed at how much time my *voisin*, the delivery men, the plumber, the electrician, and even the farmer in his field gladly give away. As if there were no end to the supply. It's as if they know there's a limitless supply of time and that's why they freely spend it on their neighbors, friends, and family.

In America, we are in such a hurry. Time is a precious commodity to be hoarded and doled out to the privileged few in measured doses. We seem to have so little time that we must cram as many things into a minute as we possibly can. We zip down the freeway, eating fast food while chatting on our hands-free cell phones. There, we didn't waste a moment of it.

How do you tell an American why you are leaving? If they're choosing to stay, then they probably couldn't understand. They're looking at the same thing you are, but they don't see it. They can't see the cage, that's what separates them from the rat. They can look right at it and never see it.

On the plane home, I sat across the aisle from a French woman, Pascale, now living in Los Angeles. As a child, she'd had terrible eczema. Like Natalie, she had also been taken to a healer. It worked for over twenty years, she told me, until she moved to Los Angeles. Now, it had returned.

To the bewilderment of the Americans sitting around us, we discussed the two healers and their methods, contemplating the source of their power. I told Pascale that, as we were leaving from the second treatment, I looked up at the magnificent church. The ancient stained-glass window—the window facing the healer's home—was the depiction of a figure, presumably Jesus. He was holding his hands outstretched toward someone, a golden ray of glass, like a beam, extending from his hands. It was an illuminated image of the very thing the healer had just performed on Natalie.

The healer, watching me and sensing I had made the connection, laughed and excitedly rattled off something in French that I could not translate. But I knew what he was saying. I could tell by the look in his eyes. I pointed at the window. *"C'est que vous faîtes?"* It is what you do?

He smiled knowingly. *"Eh, oui."*

Pascale was from the Basque country and knew the Dordogne. It was beautiful, a wonderful place to raise a child. She confessed that she was concerned for her own young children. She, too, had contemplated moving her family back to France, but it seemed like an impossible dream until now. Buoyed by our actions and the time she had just spent with her family in southern France, by the time we landed, Pascale was determined to raise her children in a land that was *calme et tranquille.*

Pascale's description of family life in her little village reminded me of life in the Dordogne. The main difference in our countries, we agreed, is the amount of time the French devote to their friends, neighbors, and family. The *joie de vie,* the joy of life. The French not only know the importance of enjoying life, they had the time to do it.

"My friends in Los Angeles," she said, "I'm lucky to see them once or twice a month. They are all so busy. Too busy making money to spend time with their friends."

It was, in the end, leaving our friends that would be the most difficult part of moving. But Pascale's words echoed inside me. She was right, I loved my friends, but with their jobs, their children, and their hectic schedules, I rarely saw them. Only half-jokingly, Pascale said that I will see more of them when I move to the Dordogne.

The second most difficult part of moving was going to be learning the language. As we sat down for our lesson, I was chastised by our *professeur.*

"Beeell. Why did you hire this British *maître d'ouevre*—good word, by the way."

"Well, because I—"

She folded her arms for emphasis and said, "Because you'd seen her work?"

"No."

She arched her eyebrows and turned her head, looking at me nearly in profile. "Because you checked her references?"

"Well, no."

"Beeell! Don't tell me you hired her because she spoke English?!"

I nodded in embarrassment. Yes, I admitted, I preferred speaking English. French is beautiful to listen to, but when it came time to discuss slanted ceilings and cracked rooms, I'd rather be sarcastic in English than fumbling for French.

—{ HER STORY }—

~~CHAPITRE VINGT-ET-DEUX~~
CHAPTER TWENTY-TWO

AHHHHH!

"Are you ready for the big move?" everyone asked.

Of course not! No matter how much preparation we had done, no matter how much investigation, we would never be ready. It's kind of like jumping out of an airplane, except instead of "Geronimo," you shriek, "Oh, shit!"

In the whirlwind of movers coming in and out, Bill took me aside. "Don't let them touch those boxes."

"Which boxes?" I wrung my hands as the stoned moving crew breathed down our necks, giving me something of a second-hand high. There was a selection of boxes that we were going to send by Fed-Ex with the items we would need shortly upon arrival; everything else was going into storage while the house was renovated.

"The ones in the corner."

These were the boxes with Bill's pages on his most recent book—the one you are reading right now. As our moving day rapidly approached, Bill had spent most of his time recording TV shows for us to have something to watch in France, more or less avoiding the actual packing process. (But this was years before the latest hit movies were right there on your iPhone. You have no idea how those *Seinfeld* reruns lightened our spirits in the days to come!)

Of course, no matter how many times I warned the movers, one of "those boxes" ended up missing. Bill was not happy, to say the least. Neither was Chief, the Head Mover, who was, unfortunately, also the chief stoner.

"I need that box," Bill told him. "It was never supposed to be loaded onto the truck."

"Well, it is now," was the response.

"All of this stuff is going into storage in France—for who knows how long. So, we're going to need to find that box."

They resisted, ganging up on Bill at the doorstep, all five of them, including the tough Lady Mover. As the shouting escalated, I got between them.

"I have a baby in here. Cut it out!"

I slammed the door in their faces, preventing the foreshadowed pummeling of my husband.

I looked out the door shortly thereafter, they were nowhere to be seen, but the truck was still parked out front. At least they hadn't left. About a half hour later, the "box" showed up on the doorstep and the Lady Mover had taken the place of her stoned husband. Chief, who we fortunately saw little more of, was now dosed into a calm oblivion, so much so that he had dropped one of his bottles of pills on the steps.

It isn't simple for anyone to coordinate the packing up of a whole household and moving it 10,000 miles to France, but our situation was a bit complicated. We were going to put most everything on a container and into storage; little did we know that it would stay there for almost two years!

The thirty or so boxes we were shipping, some Fed-Ex, some regular mail, became the real challenge. Being a photographer/writer, I had a lot of stuff. Bill, being a writer and a musician, also had a lot of stuff. Then there was Natalie's stuff. Stuff, stuff, stuff, precious things that we had to have with us when we arrived or shortly thereafter.

I thought I had it all planned out. The afternoon before the day we had to leave, my friend Mary Jo, my babysitter/housekeeper in her borrowed van, and I made our caravan down to the post office. Luckily, before I started unloading, I went in to talk to the man behind the counter. He looked at me over his glasses in disbelief when I told him that I had thirty boxes all in need of paperwork in order to ship to France. He looked up at the clock, it was four-thirty; thirty minutes before closing. He looked at me like I was crazy, "No way. Come back tomorrow and start filling out the forms tonight, one for each package." He stated emphatically. Tomorrow? The day we were to fly?!

However, the next day, by the time we got the boxes off—deciding which ones to send quickly, which ones we could wait for—we were going to miss our plane. I rescheduled the flight for the following morning, departing LAX at 9:00 am. We had kept a futon, a crib, some dishes, and odds and ends to get us through the last night. We had contemplated staying in a hotel, but we wanted to spend our last night in America in our own home, the home we had lived in for ten years.

By this time, I was emotionally and physically spent, but Bill had other ideas.

"We have to make love the last night in our home."

"We do?" I asked.

"Oh, honey . . ."

But being a trooper, I let him try and get me in the mood. He was succeeding when around midnight we heard voices coming from the front yard. Burglars? We wondered. Well, sort of. It was Bill's sister Jac who was coming by to get his car and some plants we told her she could have. She and his nephew were in the process of trying to drag an antique urn, which she had mistakenly thought was hers to take, down the front stairs when we called out, startling her. Jac had thought we'd be gone and was glad to see us, ready to visit. Bill, on the other hand, had other plans. By the time they left it was one o'clock and we had to leave for the airport at six. We would have to wait and christen our new home in France. Our new home, Villa Page.

The next morning, we rushed around getting the last bits and pieces—everything out of the house, leaving it in front of our garage, much to our neighbor's distain, I'm sure. Whatever the gardener didn't want, the vultures would descend and take away.

The taxi waited patiently, the driver did not. This was it, the moment we had been planning for years. The last goodbye. Bill was the last one out, of course. The driver helped me get the packed-to-the-brim suitcases down the stairs. We had weighed them and they were right on the edge of passing. They would understand, wouldn't they? We were leaving our home and moving to another country, don't you get a few pounds tolerance for that?

I got Natalie situated in her car seat. The driver looked at his watch and back up at the house. I went up a few stairs, here Bill came. Was that a tear I saw? It must have been a huge responsibility to be the one who was steering this boat. He gave me a weak smile as he came down the stairs and shut the gate for the last time. We had lived there ten years and it was our pride and joy; we had restored the house to its present glory and it would always have a solid hold on our hearts.

We piled into the taxi and fastened our seat belts. I was openly crying now, as was Bill. When the taxi pulled away, I looked at the house as it set on its imposing position up in the trees. Did we really know what we were doing, leaving our home, our friends and family, our country?

Oh, well, here goes nothing . . . Geronimo! (Oh, *merde!*)

―{ BOOK TWO }―

BONJOUR, VILLA PAGE!

Part two in the series tells the often hilarious, frequently terrifying, unbelievably challenging, yet ultimately life-affirming story of the Royce family as they sell their home in Hollywood, say good-bye to their friends and family, and move to their Dream Life in France.

Well, *his* Dream anyway.

Villa Page

The Dordogne River – our backyard

The Dordogne River from Domme

Carroll O'Connor at our wedding

The village of Beynac

Specialties of the Périgord

A hot-air balloon lands across the road

The enchanting village of Limeuil

Swan Island in Allas-les-Mines

Micheltorena home in Los Angeles – the gazebo

Micheltorena home in Los Angeles

The Royce family in Los Angeles

The River Dronne in Bourdeilles

Sunflowers in Vitrac

Farmer's home in Limeuil

Alley view in La Roque-Gageac

The Renaissance town of Sarlat at Christmas

Typical Périgordian borie

The stunning vertical village of Rocamadour at sunrise

Café de Sauve Terre—Allas-les-Mines

Sketch for the Café de Sauve Terre Wine Bar

The view of Castelnaud from Castle Beynac

Chévre at the Marché

La Poste—Beynac

Cave au vin – Le Moulin du Roc Hotel

Dessert at Moulin du Roc

Le Moulin du Roc Hotel – bridge

Le Moulin du Roc Hotel – mill wheel

The Château Montfort at sunset

The Vitrac Bridge

Château de Castelnaud-la-Chapelle

Château Milandes

The canals of Brantôme

A church in the mist

The gates to a château in Domme

The ruins of a church in Saint-Émilion

A castle in Périgord Vert

A secret garden in St. Cyprien

A pigeonnier in Allas-les-Mines

The terrace at Villa Page

Steps built into the cliffside leading to the river at Villa Page

The covered porch at Villa Page

"Porte-cochère" at Villa Page

ABOUT THE AUTHORS

CYNTHIA ROYCE, whose nom-de-plume is Cynthia Deming, has written for the stage and the screen. Her first play, *Huddled Masses*, was a collaboration with her husband-to-be. Thus, began a partnership that has lasted thirty-five years. At the peak of her writing career, the Executive Creative Consultant  walked away from television to devote herself to photography. Her success as a travel writer/photographer led to teaching assignments in both America and France, where she taught at Downe House, a prestigious boarding school in the Dordogne.

WILLIAM J. ROYCE is an award-winning author who has written for stage and screen. He is the writer/director of the hit romantic comedy, *A Fine Romance*, and author of The Tom Sullivan Mysteries. His television credits include the Emmy Award-winning series *Murder,*  *She Wrote*; *Diagnosis: Murder*; and *In the Heat of the Night*.

www.ingramcontent.com/pod-product-compliance
Lightning Source LLC
Chambersburg PA
CBHW040313170426
43195CB00020B/2954